EDUCATED BUT
UNPREPARED

A PRACTICAL RESET FOR HIGH-ACHIEVERS NAVIGATING CHANGE WITHOUT LOSING THEMSELVES

DR. JADA L. JONES

This book is dedicated to:

The ones carrying silent battles, may these words remind you that your strength has always been enough.

Every soul who has ever felt unseen, this is your invitation to come home to yourself.

The leaders who forgot they were human first.

The ones who kept pushing when what they really needed was permission to pause.

Those who dare to begin again, even when the world expects them to keep going.

TABLE OF CONTENTS

Chapter One

I Had All the Credentials, But None of the Capacity

On paper, I was unstoppable.

I had been forged in the crucibles of elite systems. My professional identity was built on military service, higher education, and the unforgiving school of real-world leadership. My résumé spoke fluently in accolades: U.S. Army Chief Warrant Officer, Cyber Operations Advisor, Leadership Strategist, Human Behavior Analyst, Author, Entrepreneur, and Mother. I was the person people called when failure wasn't an option, the calm in the storm, the strategist in the fire, the leader who could bend chaos into order.

But no credential prepared me for the night I sat alone in my room, trying to process a breast cancer diagnosis while still reporting for all the duties I had sworn to uphold: mentoring soldiers, advising leaders, parenting, making life-or-death decisions, all while quietly carrying a battle no uniform could shield me from. That uniform then became a prison. I wasn't just physically exposed; I was emotionally bare.

It didn't prepare me for the numbness that followed losing someone I loved, with no time to grieve. It certainly didn't prepare me for the disorientation I felt every night after taking the uniform off, when I came face-to-face with myself.

You see, I was educated in systems but unprepared for the soul work. I could master processes, people, and performance under pressure, but when it came to grief, identity, or emotional reckoning, I was profoundly unequipped.

And here's the truth no resume tells you: so are most of us.

Take the story of Sheryl Sandberg, former COO of Meta. She faced something similar. After her husband died unexpectedly, she returned to work in one of the most powerful roles in tech, carrying grief no training could prepare her for. Instead of hiding her pain, she wrote what became Option B, a Facebook post that said:

"I think there are two ways through the loss of a love … You can rock yourself back and forth by the void … or you can try to find meaning."

She chose meaning. And in doing so, she redefined what leadership looks like, showing up not as invulnerable but as human. That vulnerability became a movement, teaching many of us that you can still lead, even amid heartbreak.

See, we all want to create a comfortable environment for ourselves, our families, and our loved ones. We're taught that if we follow the rules, play it safe, collect the degrees, and climb the ladder, life will reward us with stability, respect, and fulfillment. And for a time, it does. Until one day you wake up in a house full of things you don't need, surrounded by people who drain you, working in a role your soul never chose.

At first, the noise keeps you distracted. The promotions. The pay raises. The validation. It feels like success, until the silence creeps in. Until the Freaky Friday effect wears off and you realize you're living someone else's life. That's when depression knocks. That's when anxiety whispers that you've been compensating for something you didn't even realize you lost.

If you're lucky, clarity strikes. But it doesn't come wrapped in serenity and wisdom. It hits like a violent punch to the gut. You realize the "success" you've been chasing is society's definition, not yours. You're not filled with peace; you're filled with dread, regret, and questions that won't let you sleep:

What if I've wasted years living for recognition instead of purpose?

What if no one was watching, would I still be doing this?

Why am I so obsessed with their approval?

The answers don't come easy. They sound something like: *Because I don't want to fail. Because I'm afraid to walk away from what's comfortable. Because I need validation to quiet my insecurities.*

Because if I step into my truth, I might lose the image I've worked so hard to maintain.

Bingo. That's ego talking.

And here's the dangerous part: ego will convince you it's your identity. It will fight tooth and nail to keep its power. It will whisper that *your worth is tied to your titles, your image, your applause.* It will keep you bound to the expectations of others, afraid to stand out, afraid to offend, afraid to want more than the safe script.

But here's the reality: you are not your ego.

Ego is the voice that tells you to *stay small while pretending you're living big.* It is the gatekeeper between who you are and who you could become. And unless you confront it, ego will win. It will steal your time, your peace, and eventually your sense of self.

The Disconnected Leader

At 2:17 a.m., a Fortune 500 CEO sat alone in his office, the glow of his laptop casting long shadows on the walls. Hours earlier, he had closed the biggest deal of his career, a milestone that should have felt like triumph. But instead of raising a glass or pausing to reflect, his fingers were already racing across the keyboard, sketching out the strategy for the next quarter. No celebration. No acknowledgment of victory. Just one question repeating in his mind: *What's next?*

This scene isn't rare; it's the norm. We live under the false pretense that in order for us to succeed, or even to be perceived as successful, we must remain in constant motion. The dream commands that we achieve. "The hustle never dies." "The grind never stops." These aren't just catchy mantras anymore; they've become conditions of success itself. They flood our psyche, whispering that *our worth is measured entirely by how much we produce, how quickly we move, and how big the results look to others.*

Stillness has no seat at the table. To pause is to risk irrelevance. To stop is to fall behind. In this culture, productivity is more than a goal; it's a weapon wielded against our own sense of identity. Anything less than exceptional is branded as unacceptable. And so the moment we reach a goal, no matter how monumental, it's not a place of rest or gratitude. It's simply a launchpad for the question: *What's next?*

This is the myth of the glorified leader: that relentless motion equals true success. And it's a myth perpetuated by how we reward leadership. We celebrate reactivity, praising those who can produce more under tighter deadlines with fewer resources, never stopping to ask if this pace is sustainable or if it's even meaningful.

The truth is this obsession with constant output isn't new. It's deeply entrenched in history. As societies industrialized, arduous work became a badge of honor. Productivity wasn't just necessary; it was framed as virtuous. Individuals surrendered autonomy, reducing labor to faceless output. The joy of creation, the spark of genius, even the simple breath of fresh air, all were replaced by the demand to produce more, faster.

And so here we are, in a world where reactive leadership is overvalued, where high productivity is demanded at any cost. Work hours stretch longer. Pressure grows tighter. The grind does not slow, and still, we refuse to name the cost.

Maybe you've felt it too. The inability to fully enjoy your successes. The fear that *maybe* you don't belong. The conviction that *you're an impostor pretending* to hold it together. The nagging question of whether *your purpose is truly yours or simply shaped by someone else's demands.* You feel trapped, like sprinting on a treadmill that never moves you forward. No matter how hard you run, you're right back where you started.

But the awakening we need isn't about rejecting ambition or abandoning excellence. It's about reclaiming what we've forgotten, that our value doesn't lie solely in output. That leadership is more than constant motion. That success without self is just another form of loss.

To move beyond this cycle is not to escape, but to recover what is already within us: clarity, purpose, and the courage to ask different questions. Not *What's next?* but *Why this? Not How much more? but What truly matters?*

Because the truth is, the world will always press forward, but you don't have to lose yourself trying to keep up.

When Excellence Becomes a Mask

High-performance culture harbors the perilous fallacy that professional mastery equates to mastery of life itself. External excellence often conceals profound internal dissonance, and I learned this at the cost of an inner fracture. We are schooled in execution, but rarely in the art of surrender. True readiness is not flawless strategy; it's the resilience to stay grounded when everything beneath you is crumbling.

I know this firsthand. For years, I wore excellence like armor, until it became my mask. I wasn't leading from freedom; I was leading from fear. I was a perfectionist, and for a long time I believed that was something to be proud of. But when excellence becomes distressing, it shifts from aspiration to burden. It becomes a mask, worn not to inspire but to conceal.

This illusion of control is both prison and refuge. It promises safety while quietly eroding your sense of self. You no longer know where the titles end and where you begin. And it is not sustainable. To live fully, we must relinquish the fantasy of absolute control and create space to breathe, realign, and rediscover what it means to lead, not just with competence but with authenticity.

Check-In Moment: Be Honest With Yourself

- Who have I trained the world to see me as—and what is the cost of keeping that performance alive?

- Which part of me is silently screaming for rest, but I keep silencing with busyness or "strength"?

- What am I calling discipline or toughness that is really just emotional suppression?

No judgment. Just truth.

Because the goal of this book isn't to make you more impressive. It's to make you more integrated. To stop pretending you're fine when you're not. To stop leading from burnout and start leading from alignment.

This isn't about powering through anymore.

It's about pausing.

It's about breathing.

It's about coming home to yourself.

And that's where our journey begins.

Chapter Two

The Education They Never Gave Us

The Preparation Paradox

Traditional education, whether military academies, graduate schools, or professional development programs, excels at preparing us for external mastery. We learn to analyze, strategize, and execute with precision. We become experts at managing projects, leading teams, and delivering outcomes. But somewhere in all that credential accumulation, we miss the most essential education of all: how to navigate our own humanity when life strips away everything we think defines us.

I once sat across from a soldier who had just returned from deployment. He had survived firefights, executed missions flawlessly, and earned the kind of commendations that made others whisper his name with respect. Yet sitting in that chair, away from the uniform and the accolades, he confessed in a whisper I'll never forget:

"Ma'am, I can brief generals without breaking a sweat. But I don't know how to go home and look my daughter in the eye. I don't know how to be present without feeling like I'm failing."

His words crystallized what I was living: we were both trained for external mastery, yet neither of us had been prepared for the quiet, interior battles, the ones that happen when the uniform comes off and the roles fall.

Because I too could navigate chaos in the professional arena, yet I couldn't recognize my own burnout until my body staged a full-on rebellion. For months, I ignored the signals: fatigue I brushed off as "normal," sleepless nights I masked with coffee, and a creeping numbness I refused to name. I carried it all like an invisible rucksack, each unprocessed emotion and unmet need another weight strapped to my shoulders. The heavier it got, the more I convinced myself to just tighten the straps and keep moving. I defaulted to what training had always rewarded: endure, lead, and push through.

Different battlefield, same blind spot.

This is the educated professional's paradox: we become so skilled at external competence that we remain novices at internal navigation. We're trained for the battlefield, the boardroom, the classroom, the crisis, but rarely for the silence of our own souls when the roles fall away.

The Four Critical Gaps in Professional Education
Gap#1: Identity Beyond Performance

- **What They Taught Us:** How to excel in roles–student, employee, leader, expert

- **What They Didn't Teach Us:** Who we are when we're not performing

In military training, your identity becomes inseparable from your rank and mission. In graduate school, you're defined by your research and academic standing. In corporate environments, you are your job title and performance metrics. This creates what I call "credential identity," a sense of self that exists only in relation to external achievements.

I'll never forget the moment someone asked me to introduce myself without mentioning my job, rank, or achievements. It was at a leadership retreat, a casual circle of people sitting in folding chairs. The facilitator smiled and said, *"Tell us who you are without using your title."*

Easy, I thought. I've introduced myself hundreds of times. But as the person next to me spoke about being a curious traveler, a proud aunt, and a lover of jazz, my mind went blank. When it was my turn, I froze.

I opened my mouth and nothing came out. Without my résumé to hide behind, I didn't know who I was. My throat tightened, my palms got sweaty, and I gave the safest, flattest answer I could manage: *"I'm Jada."* Even that sounded foreign, like a placeholder for a person I hadn't met yet.

11

The silence after my answer felt heavier than any military debriefing I'd ever sat through. That's when it hit me: twenty years of education had taught me to perform an identity, but never to cultivate one. I knew how to be what the world needed, but I had no idea how to just be.

The problem emerges during transitions. When the role changes, the promotion doesn't come, or the mission ends, we experience what feels like identity death. We never learned that we are not what we do; we are who we choose to be underneath all the doing.

Gap #2: Emotional Navigation Under Pressure

- **What They Taught Us:** How to manage external stress and lead others through crisis

- **What They Didn't Teach Us:** How to process our own emotional landscape during upheaval

Professional education trains us to compartmentalize. In the military, you learn to suppress fear to complete the mission. In healthcare, you manage life-and-death situations while remaining clinically detached. In corporate leadership, you project confidence even when the numbers are terrifying.

This emotional compartmentalization becomes so automatic that we lose access to our own feelings. We can read a room, manage a team's morale, and navigate organizational politics, but we can't identify what we're feeling or why.

When I received my cancer diagnosis, my immediate response wasn't fear or grief; it was logistics. I braced myself for impact. But instead of breaking down, my brain snapped *into operations mode. I didn't cry. I didn't scream. I didn't even ask, Why me? My first words were: What's the treatment timeline? How do I maintain my commitments? Can I schedule surgery around school semesters, or even my son's schedule?* I had been so thoroughly trained to manage external challenges that I couldn't access my own human response to a life-threatening illness.

That response wasn't resilience; it was conditioning. I defaulted to logistics because that's what I had been trained to do: control, plan, execute. I could map out scenarios, but I couldn't sit in my own fear long enough to acknowledge it. I was leading my illness like it was a mission instead of feeling it like it was my life.

Later, I realized that was the real blind spot. Education had taught me how to lead through external chaos, but not how to navigate my own internal storm. It prepared me to be the calm in everyone else's crisis, but not to process my own grief, anger, or vulnerability.

Gap #3: Thriving in Ambiguity

- **What They Taught Us:** How to solve problems with clear parameters and measurable outcomes

- **What They Didn't Teach Us:** How to navigate uncertainty with grace and wisdom

Dr. Jada l. Jones

Professional education often trains us to believe there are always solutions, strategies, and control. But when life fractures expectations, through identity shifts, health crises, or spiritual awakenings, these frameworks begin to crumble. Those moments demand ambiguous courage, not action plans. They require a different kind of intelligence, one that can hold paradox, embrace uncertainty, and find meaning in the midst of not knowing.

I spent my career planning for every contingency. Yet when I faced the gap between who I was and who I hoped to become, no blueprint brought clarity. My education taught me to find answers, but life asked me to live the questions. It was as if I was protecting the message when, in truth, the message was me becoming the message. My story, my energy, my transformation were the answers to all my questions.

This reminds me of the leadership teachings of John Maxwell, who emphasizes that real leadership isn't about titles or having all the answers, but about influence and authenticity. As he's pointed out, "Just because someone has a title doesn't mean that person is a leader."

In ambiguity, leadership isn't found in external definition, but in presence, in being enough even without clarity. That's the kind of maturity ambiguity demands: the ability to hold space when there are no answers, to lead from presence when strategy fails.

14

Gap #4: Sustainable Wholeness vs. Impressive Performance

- **What They Taught Us:** How to optimize, achieve, and exceed expectations

- **What They Didn't Teach Us:** How to exist, rest, and create from a place of enoughness

The hidden curriculum of high achievement is that your worth equals your output. More credentials, higher performance, greater recognition, these become the metrics by which we measure not just our success, but our value as human beings.

This creates what I call "performance addiction," the inability to exist without producing, to be present without achieving, to rest without guilt. We become human doings instead of human beings, and our bodies, relationships, and spirit eventually demand an accounting.

Here's the paradox: the very education that gave us mastery in performance often left us novices at wholeness. We know how to impress, but not how to sustain.

Tony Robbins has spoken candidly about this paradox. Early in his career, he was working nonstop with seminars, coaching, media, and writing, all in the pursuit of helping millions of people transform their lives. Yet he admitted that at one point his relentless schedule left him depleted, even though the world saw him as wildly successful. Robbins eventually realized that true success wasn't about endless output, but about state management, cultivating energy, presence, and balance so that achievement flows from vitality rather than exhaustion.

That principle, success without sacrifice, is the antidote to performance addiction. We must learn that rest is not weakness but wisdom, and that the foundation of sustainable achievement is alignment, not overextension.

The education system that created our success becomes the prison that contains our growth. We know how to be impressive, but we've forgotten how to be whole.

The Competence-Confidence Trap

Here's the cruelest irony: the very education that gives us confidence in professional settings often creates profound insecurity in personal ones. We're accustomed to being the expert, the one with answers, the person others turn to for guidance. When life presents challenges that can't be solved with our professional toolkit, we don't just feel confused, we feel incompetent.

I remember sitting in a counseling session not long after my diagnosis. The therapist asked me a simple question: "How are you feeling?" Without missing a beat, I launched into a detailed response about my medical appointments, my work obligations, and how I was planning to manage the disruption. She paused, then repeated the question, this time slower: "No, how are you feeling?"

And that's when I realized: I didn't even have words for my own emotions. I was fluent in leading others, but illiterate in leading myself. Years of training had taught me to analyze, to strategize, to lead, but not to sit with my own humanity. That's the competence–confidence trap.

It keeps high achievers stuck longer than necessary. We resist seeking help because we're supposed to be the helpers. We avoid admitting uncertainty because our careers depend on projecting confidence. We struggle to become beginners again in the school of our own lives.

I was a behavioral analyst who couldn't analyze her own behavior. A leadership trainer who couldn't lead herself through critical transitions. That gap between my professional competence and my personal confusion felt like a shameful secret, when in truth, it was simply part of being human.

But clarity and momentum only come when we stop branding the parts and start owning the whole. When I finally admitted I didn't have all the answers, it didn't make me less of a leader. It made me more real, more accessible, more whole.

The next level of your life won't require a rebrand. It won't be about proving you're smart enough, strong enough, or polished enough. It will require a reintroduction of you, to you. Because the world doesn't need another perfect expert. It needs a whole human willing to show up as they are.

And when you do that, you give others permission to do the same.

The Real-Life Education Looks Like

The education we need for navigating human complexity can't be found in any curriculum; it must be lived, felt, and integrated through experience. It requires what I call "embodied learning," knowledge that settles into your bones, not just your brain. It shows up in the breath you finally release after years of holding it in, in the calm that returns after a season of panic, in the laughter that bubbles up when you thought joy was impossible. No institution can give you that. Life has to teach it to you.

Lesson 1: Identity Integration

Learning that you are both your professional competence and your human complexity. You don't have to choose between being successful and being authentic; you can be both, but it requires integration rather than compartmentalization.

Lesson 2: Emotional Intelligence 2.0

Moving beyond managing other people's emotions to actually feeling and processing your own. This isn't just a soft skill; it's essential intelligence for navigating life's inevitable transitions.

For years, I could walk into any room and name everyone else's emotions. Yet if someone asked me, "How do you feel?" I had nothing. The day I finally learned to say, "I feel scared," out loud was the day fear lost its grip. Naming what's inside you doesn't make you weak; it makes you free.

Lesson 3: Uncertainty as Teacher

Recognizing that not knowing isn't a problem to be solved but the space to be inhabited. The ability to remain present and resourceful in ambiguity becomes a crucial life skill.

Lesson 4: Sustainable Success

Understanding that true achievement isn't about proving your worth; it's about expressing your gifts from a place of wholeness rather than emptiness.

I had to redefine success from being the most efficient strategist or decorated leader to being a healthy mother who could sit on the floor and laugh with her son without guilt. That moment of unmeasured joy reminded me that the world doesn't just need your output, it needs your presence.

The Continuing Education Requirement

The most successful professionals know that real education never ends; it evolves. Just as we update our technical skills and industry knowledge, we must develop our capacity for personal navigation and authentic leadership.

Formal education ends with a diploma. Real education begins with disruption. One is measured in credits; the other is measured in scars, tears, and breakthroughs. One makes you competent; the other makes you whole.

This isn't about abandoning your credentials or diminishing your achievement. It's about realizing the education they gave us was never supposed to be the end; it was only the foundation. The real curriculum is life itself. And whether you like it or not, class has already started.

Check-In Moment: Your Education Gap Assessment

Pause here. Every student eventually hits the test they weren't taught to take. This is yours.

- What did your education prepare you to handle exceptionally well?

- Where do you feel most confident and competent?

- When have you felt underprepared despite your credentials?

- What challenges has life thrown at you that no classroom prepared you for?

- If you wrote the syllabus for "Life Navigation 101," what would the first lessons be?

This isn't about criticizing your education; it's about acknowledging its limits so you can consciously develop the wisdom it couldn't provide.

Because the goal isn't to be perfectly prepared for everything.

The goal is to be courageously present for anything.

And the truth is, that starts now.

Chapter Three

When Intelligence Isn't Enough

I used to believe that intelligence was a form of immunity, that if I studied hard enough, planned thoroughly enough, and stayed disciplined enough, I could outsmart life's inevitable challenges. My advanced degrees and certifications felt like protective armor, my behavioral analysis training like a crystal ball, my military discipline like an unbreachable fortress.

I was wrong.

Intelligence, I learned, is not protection from the human experience. It's just a different way of moving through it. And sometimes, it's the very thing that blinds us to what our bodies, hearts, and spirits are desperately trying to tell us.

The Myth of Intellectual Immunity

High achievers often suffer from what I call "credential confidence," the unconscious belief that our education and expertise make us exempt from the messier aspects of being human. We think our intelligence should protect us from making poor decisions, our training should shield us from emotional overwhelm, our discipline should prevent us from falling apart.

This myth is particularly seductive for those of us trained in fields related to human behavior, health, or performance. I could teach workshops on stress management while ignoring my own stress signals. I could analyze other people's self-destructive patterns while engaging in my own. I could lead others through crisis while privately unraveling.

The irony is that our intelligence often becomes the very mechanism we use to rationalize our denial. We're smart enough to explain away the symptoms, educated enough to convince ourselves we know better, disciplined enough to power through when our bodies are begging us to stop. Unfortunately, none of that matters when your nervous system is short-circuiting and your spirit is depleted. No amount of training and no number of credentials can protect you from a body that has been running on empty for far longer than was sustainable.

The Day My Body Said "Enough"

I woke up one day that started like any other day in what I thought was a life well managed. I had my routines, my systems, my balance of professional demands and personal maintenance. On paper, I was the picture of high-functioning success.

But my body knew better.

It wasn't dramatic, no collapse, no emergency, no obvious crisis. Just a persistent fogginess that caffeine couldn't clear, an exhaustion that sleep didn't touch, and a subtle but undeniable sense that something fundamental was off. My skin was breaking out like a teenager despite my skincare routine. My energy felt perpetually low despite my consistent exercise regimen.

At first, I did what every intelligent person does: I diagnosed myself. Too much work stress, probably. Not enough water. Maybe I was fighting off a virus. I ran through my mental checklist of logical explanations and rational solutions. I optimized my schedule, adjusted my nutrition, doubled down on my wellness routines.

The symptoms persisted.

Then I did what every person does when self-diagnosis fails: I researched. I consulted medical websites, cross-referenced symptoms, built probabilistic models in my head about what might be wrong and how to fix it. I approached my own health like a strategic problem to be solved.

That would all change within a couple of weeks. I had scheduled doctor's appointments to get evaluated. After that, my days consisted of uncertainty, worry, and fear. But then days turned into weeks. A few weeks later, I was sitting in a doctor's office getting my results.

And then came the diagnosis: "You have breast cancer, not just one tumor but two that are different from each other."

Those are the words that can and will change your life and everything you've known up until then. It's a wrecking ball, and once you're hit with it, there's nothing left standing on the other side. Whatever you expect from hearing those words doesn't even begin to compare to the actual out-of-body experience that follows. The world evaporates in a haze, your surroundings turn into a blur, and you feel like everything you've built, everything you've made yourself into, is collapsing right beneath your feet.

The moment of diagnosis is such a defining one, a rarity that nobody expects to go through. You think to yourself, it's unnatural, the same way it is when parents outlive their children, the same way when the mother of diseases whisks your loved ones away. Your brain is in a state of shock and disbelief, a thousand ideas flashing through in shambles, trying to grasp at straws.

No matter what imagery I use, no matter how eloquent I try to be, I truly believe I cannot capture how agonizing and excruciating it was to hear those words. The heartbreak, the trauma, the soaring pain. But I've done so much to get to where I am. *But I've sacrificed so much. But I'm still young. But what about my child...*

This is the kind of mental wiring we develop when we have built our entire identity around problem-solving. I was used to holding it together, but here's what I had to confront: this art of pushing through that took me years to master had only drowned the agonizing screams of my body. I had to readjust my mindset and attune myself to my body's needs.

When Credentials Become Crutches

In the moment of diagnosis, my immediate response wasn't human; it was professional. Even as the word "cancer" hung in the air like a question mark over everything I thought I knew about my life, my mind defaulted to the only mode it knew: problem-solving.

I was trying to project-manage my own mortality.

This is what happens when intelligence becomes our primary coping mechanism: we lose access to other, equally important ways of processing life's challenges. We think our way through experiences that require feeling, analyze situations that call for surrender, and strategize responses to circumstances that demand presence.

My military training had taught me to maintain mission focus under pressure. My academic background had trained me to research and analyze before acting. My professional development had rewarded my ability to stay calm and competent in crisis. These were all valuable skills that had served me well in countless situations.

But cancer didn't care about my credentials.

The Smart Person's Health Paradox

Here's what I discovered: as I mentioned earlier, intelligent people often make terrible health decisions not despite their intelligence, but because of it. We're skilled enough to rationalize away symptoms, educated enough to self-diagnose incorrectly, disciplined enough to push through warning signs that should stop us in our tracks.

We treat our bodies like poorly performing assets in need of optimization rather than wise partners deserving of attention. We expect our physical selves to comply with our mental demands, to operate according to our schedules, to respond to our productivity routines.

When our bodies resist, through illness, exhaustion, or breakdown, we experience it as a personal failure rather than an inevitable consequence of treating ourselves like machines that can be upgraded instead of humans that need to be honored.

The Three Stages of Intelligent Denial

Stage 1: Rational Explanation

- *"This is just stress. I can manage stress. I have strategies for stress."*

27

We intellectualize symptoms, create logical frameworks for why we feel terrible, and implement evidence-based solutions that work for other people but somehow don't work for us.

Stage 2: Strategic Optimization

- *"I need better systems. More efficiency. Improved routines."*

When the rational explanations fail, we double down on control. We optimize our calendars, biohack our routines, and implement new productivity methods. We approach our breaking point like a business problem that can be solved with better management.

Stage 3: Competent Collapse

- *"I can handle this. I just need to be smarter about it."*

Even when our bodies force a crisis, we maintain the illusion that our intelligence can manage our way out. We research our conditions extensively, become experts in our own right, and try to be the most educated patients our doctors have ever seen.

The Body's Rebellion Against Performance

Our bodies are not impressed by our degrees. They don't care about our plans or performance reviews. They operate according to ancient wisdom that predates our modern education, and when we ignore that wisdom long enough, they eventually demand our attention through illness, exhaustion, or breakdown.

Cancer was my body's way of saying, "We need to talk."

For years, I had been running on what I call "achievement adrenaline," the constant low-level stress of striving, proving, and performing. I fueled myself with caffeine and determination, sustained myself with purpose and discipline, and convinced myself that was what strength looked like.

My body disagreed.

The fatigue wasn't laziness; it was wisdom. The brain fog wasn't incompetence; it was protection. The physical symptoms I had been trying to manage were actually messages I had been refusing to receive.

My immune system, it turned out, was exhausted from protecting me not just from external threats, but from the internal demands I had been placing on it for years.

Beyond Mind Over Matter

The "mind over matter" philosophy, while inspiring, can become dangerous when it encourages us to override our body's intelligence rather than integrate with it. There's a difference between mental resilience and mental tyranny, between disciplined living and body betrayal.

True intelligence includes somatic intelligence, the ability to listen to and learn from our physical experience. It means recognizing that our bodies have information our minds don't have access to, that our emotions carry data our logic can't process, and that our intuition knows things our analysis can't uncover.

This doesn't mean abandoning our analytical capabilities or dismissing the value of strategic thinking. It means expanding our definition of intelligence to include the full spectrum of human knowing.

The Integration Imperative

Recovery, from cancer, from burnout, from any crisis that forces us to confront the limits of intellectual control, requires what I call "integrated intelligence." This means learning to honor both our cognitive capabilities and our embodied wisdom.

Cognitive Intelligence: The ability to analyze, strategize, and problem-solve

Emotional Intelligence: The capacity to feel, process, and learn from our emotional experiences

Somatic Intelligence: The wisdom to listen to and respond to our body's signals

Intuitive Intelligence: The skill of accessing knowledge that comes through presence rather than analysis

When we integrate these different ways of knowing, we become not just smart but wise. We make decisions not only with our heads but with our whole selves. We lead not only with competence but with authenticity.

The Wisdom of Limitation

Perhaps the most important lesson cancer taught me was that intelligence without self-awareness is just sophisticated self-destruction, that discipline without self-compassion is just elegant self-abuse, and that achievement without alignment is just productive emptiness.

Our limitations aren't failures of intelligence; they're invitations to wisdom. When I finally stopped trying to think my way through cancer and started feeling my way through it, everything changed. I discovered that my body wasn't broken; it was communicating.

My emotions weren't weakness; they were information. My need for rest wasn't laziness; it was a requirement.

Check-In Moment: Your Intelligence Inventory

Let's pause here and get honest about how your intelligence might be both serving and limiting you:

- Where has your intelligence protected you from facing difficult truths?

31

- What symptoms or signals have you rationalized away because you "know better"?

- How has your education become a barrier to listening to other forms of wisdom?

- What would change if you trusted your body's intelligence as much as your mind's?

This isn't about becoming anti-intellectual or abandoning critical thinking. It's about recognizing that true intelligence includes the wisdom to know when thinking isn't enough.

Sometimes the smartest thing you can do is stop trying to be smart. Sometimes the most educated response is to admit you need to learn something that can't be taught in any classroom. And sometimes the highest form of intelligence is simply the courage to be human.

Chapter Four

When the Title Isn't Enough

There comes a moment in every high achiever's life when even the most illustrious titles begin to feel weightless. They no longer satisfy the soul, not because they vanish, but because you do.

For years, I wore my roles like armor, dressing in borrowed identities I thought would protect me from uncertainty. I found refuge in them: cyber advisor, strategist, integrator, behavioral analyst, veteran, mentor, mom, wife, friend. Each title told the world who I was and gave me something to hold onto when I didn't know who I was becoming. But what happens when the title isn't enough?

The danger isn't in feeling stuck; it's in staying stuck. You long to move forward, yet fear of failure chains you in place, not because you don't know where to go, what path to take, or how to advance, but because you're so anxious and overwhelmed by this new realization that making the smallest decision can push you to the brink of a mental breakdown. You know possibilities exist, but the simple act of choosing feels paralyzing.

And so, you sit. Alive but unmoving. Surrounded by color yet trapped in silence. Dreams dissolve. Promises you've broken to yourself float back like ghosts. Confidence erodes. For the first time in forever, you wonder if giving up would be easier.

You are face-to-face with long-lost dreams that seem to be evaporating into an eerie stillness without meaning, without end. The buried sorrows of those unfulfilled promises you've made to yourself surface, any glimmer of confidence you once had is eroding, and for the first time in forever, all you want to do is give up.

But here's the truth: if titles can no longer hold you, it means something deeper is calling.

The Shift I Didn't See Coming

I will never forget standing in front of the mirror one morning after taking off my uniform: no rank, no name tag, no accountability to report, just plain and unadorned me. For a split second, I didn't even recognize myself. The woman in the mirror was a stranger, or maybe I hadn't paused long enough to see her for what seemed like years.

When you've been trained to perform and produce, your identity becomes inseparable from the results you generate. The outcomes you achieve begin to shape and define your sense of self. And so the self starts to mirror the tally of its achievements. Success and failure become your reflection.

I had to ask myself, who am I without the metrics? What do I say when someone asks what I do and I don't have a ready-made title to fire back?

It is a strange paradox: to be both accomplished and completely unsure of yourself. I began to grieve a version of myself I had built, the woman who juggled it all, smiled through stress, and mistook being needed for being valuable. That grief was marked by a pervasive numbness I couldn't seem to shake at the time.

"If I am no longer that self, then what is left to claim?"

You Can Lose Yourself in Success, Too

As professionals, we tend to feel pressured to act a certain way and look a certain way, especially around others. We're taught early on to measure our worth against impossible ideals if we want to succeed in life. To compare ourselves endlessly to sisters, cousins, colleagues, strangers online. Even independence has been weaponized. Even the idea of success drilled and instilled in our brains can be incredibly limiting.

We've all been subjected to countless iterations of: "No one will care for you if you…" or "You'll never succeed if you…" Productivity became the altar. Every empty moment was something to optimize, to hustle, to monetize. Our plates overflow, yet we pile on more because "busy" has become the badge of belonging.

It's as if for each goal we set for ourselves, there's an inherent message that we can only reach it if we fit into this ideal of what a man or woman should be. More often than not, that ideal has nothing to do with the objective we seek to accomplish and everything to do with superficialities or the theater of our outward demeanor.

So we hoard successes like possessions: degrees, titles, promotions. We drop them into conversation like breadcrumbs, hoping for applause, the only legitimate form of validation we've been taught to seek that affirms our efforts. But the more we feed the hunger for approval, the more it consumes us.

No one tells you that you can lose yourself not only in love, motherhood, or toxic relationships, but also in success. I did. And only when I admitted that my autopilot life no longer aligned with the woman I was becoming did I start to breathe again.

Because here's the truth: titles tell the world what you do. They do not tell the truth about who you are.

Coming Back to Myself

We put our entire worth into the amount of work we're getting done, almost as if all of our life experiences and the moments that led us to where we are amount to nothing if we're not being productive. Nothing means anything anymore. It's all about being in constant survival mode, fight or flight. Yet life is not so black and white, and we have far more options than we think we do.

Not everything we engage in has to have an immediate outcome or result. Not everything in life is meant to be rewarding in some way or another. These public figures are always on the go, always onto the next thing, the next project, the next achievement, locked in a perpetual danse macabre with burnout.

Where they lead, we follow. We never stop to relish our accomplishments, we never stop to live in the moment, we are never truly present to appreciate the smallest details. We push the fast-forward button and run, chase success, chase other people, demand more productivity, overextend ourselves, feel the stress. We tell ourselves the stress is good, that it is our catalyst to do more and be more.

It's easy to get sucked into this toxic mindset, yet incredibly difficult to escape it. All the pressures and stresses you've subjected yourself to feel like they've become part of your intrinsic identity, to the point that you can barely tell where they end and you begin. You hold onto that survival state because it's all you've ever known, and any alternative feels intimidating or even impossible.

My wake-up call came in whispers and in floods: therapy sessions where I gave voice to my quiet parts, walks where I let my body lead for once, journaling that forced me to answer, *What do I actually want?* even when the answer scared me.

Layer by layer, I came back. To presence. To stillness. To the voice I had buried under performance. That voice reminded me of my value even when I wasn't producing. That voice told me who I was outside of roles, ranks, and recognition.

We all eventually get that wake-up call that tells us in blaring red lights that something is wrong with the way we're living. For some, that knock might be loud, while for others it could be a mere drop that spills the glass. Your body has been and still is providing you with plenty of clues that you're living in a state of misalignment.

It's time to reconnect with yourself. I should preface this by saying that this reconnection does not happen in one big moment. It's not instantaneous by any means. But find it, and you will stand at the center of your own existence.

That voice is the real authority.

Check-In Moment: Reclaim Your Identity

Pause right here. Take a breath.

Ask yourself:

- Who have I been performing as—and is it still aligned with who I am becoming?

- What part of me feels lost or hidden behind titles and responsibilities?

- If all the accolades disappeared tomorrow, what truth would still be left standing in me?

This isn't about abandoning what you've built.

It's about returning to what's real.

Because the most powerful version of you?

It isn't the one the world praises.

It's the one who knows who they are —even when no one else is watching.

Chapter Five

The Relationships I Wasn't Equipped to Lead

I could lead teams, navigate organizational politics, and help reset the team climates when the mission called for it. Yet when it came to the most important relationships in my life, starting with the one I had with myself, I found myself completely unprepared for the emotional intelligence required.

This isn't a story about relationship failure. It's about the specific challenges that high-achieving professionals face when the external training that makes us effective leaders doesn't translate to the internal and interpersonal skills that real intimacy demands.

The Professional Relationship Paradox

Military training taught me to be reliable, loyal, and mission focused. Academic training taught me to be analytical, objective, and solution oriented. Professional development taught me to be strategic, efficient, and results driven. These skills made me an exceptional colleague, leader, and team member.

They also made me terrible at receiving care during personal life challenges. I remember lying in the hospital bed after surgery, watching my family and friends struggle to help me while I struggled even more to let them. Every instinct I had as a leader told me to manage their emotions, solve their problems, and minimize their burden. I was so conditioned to be the competent one that I had no idea how to be the vulnerable one.

The very training that made me effective in professional arenas created blind spots in my personal life, blind spots I didn't recognize until crisis forced me to.

The Competence Trap in Relationships

When Professional Skills Become Personal Barriers

The Solver's Dilemma:

- *Professional training*: Identify problems and solve them efficiently.

- *Relationship reality:* Sometimes people don't need solutions—they need presence.

During my recovery and healing process, when loved ones shared their fears, my immediate instinct was to reassure them with statistics, plans, and optimistic projections. I tried to manage their anxiety instead of allowing space for their concerns. I treated their emotions as problems to be solved rather than experiences to witness.

The Manager's Burden:

- *Professional training*: Take responsibility for outcomes and team morale

- *Relationship reality:* Other people's emotions are not projects.

I became the project manager of everyone else's feelings. I downplayed symptoms to protect my family, maintained an impossible schedule to reassure coworkers, and worked tirelessly to keep others comfortable. In doing so, I abandoned my own experience. The more I managed their feelings, the more disconnected I became from my own.

The Expert's Isolation:

- *Professional training*: Maintain credibility through competence and confidence

- *Relationship reality*: Intimacy requires admitting what you don't know.

The hardest part wasn't asking for help with practical tasks; it was admitting I had no idea how to process what I was going through emotionally. I could analyze my options with precision, but I couldn't find language for my pain or ask for what I truly needed from the people who loved me.

The Emotional Intelligence Gap for High Achievers

What We Were Taught

- Reading room dynamics and morale
- Manage team emotions under stress
- Communicate strategically to influence outcomes
- Maintaining composure under pressure
- Inspire confidence in uncertainty

What Relationships Require

- Identify and express your own emotional needs
- Receive care without feeling like a burden
- Be present with someone else's pain without fixing it
- Ask for help without losing your sense of competence
- Allow others to see you as human, not just capable

The gap between these two skill sets is where many high performers struggle.

My Relationship Learning Curve

- **The Receiving**

I had spent years perfecting the art of giving: giving advice, giving support, giving solutions. But when life forced me to receive, I realized I had no practice accepting care without immediately trying to reciprocate or minimize the need.

Example: When friends brought meals during recovery, I apologized, promised to repay the favor, and minimized their effort. I couldn't simply accept care with a "thank you." Be open to receiving love from others; it's very refreshing.

- **The Vulnerability Resistance**

My military training had conditioned me to compartmentalize emotions for mission effectiveness. This served me well in certain situations but became a barrier when my personal life required emotional expression and processing.

Example: One day my mother asked how I was feeling. My response was a detailed medical update about my symptoms and plan going forward. When she pressed for my emotional experience, I didn't have words for what I was feeling because I hadn't practiced accessing or expressing those deeper layers, and part of me feared no one would understand anyway.

- **The Control Paradox**

I was accustomed to leading relationships, setting agendas, and managing dynamics. At that time, my health stripped away my ability to control the relational environment, and I had to learn how to participate in relationships where I wasn't the main influencer.

Example: Family calls about my care became projects I "coordinated" instead of moments to accept support. I turned intimacy into logistics because control felt safer, instead of simply accepting that they wanted to help. They were my angels on assignment.

Formal education and leadership training never taught me this. They gave me frameworks for team resilience, conflict resolution, and organizational success, but not for tending my own heart. I've seen this gap in the high performers I coach as well. We can manage projects, yet often struggle to manage ourselves.

Rebuilding Relationship Skills as a High Achiever

The Professional's Guide to Personal Intimacy

Skill 1: Translating Competence into Vulnerability Instead of hiding your struggles to maintain your image, practice sharing your learning process.

- *Old approach*: "I'm fine, everything's under control"

- *New approach*: "I'm figuring this out as I go, and it's harder than I expected"

Vulnerability doesn't erase competence—it humanizes it.

Skill 2: From Problem-Solving to Presence: When someone shares a struggle, reflect their feeling before suggesting solutions.

Example: When someone shares a concern, your first response is to reflect their feeling before offering any suggestions. Say, "That sounds really frustrating" before "Have you tried..."

Skill 3: From Independence to Interdependence: Reframe asking for help as relationship building rather than burden creation.

Mindset shift: "I'm giving people the opportunity to contribute to something meaningful" instead of "I'm imposing on people's time and energy"

Skill 4: From Managing to Participating Practice being a participant in your relationships rather than the director.

Example: In family discussions or friend gatherings, focus on sharing your authentic experience rather than facilitating everyone else's comfort.

The Relationship Ripple Effect

As I learned to receive love and support, something shifted: my professional relationships improved too. Vulnerability deepened my leadership. Presence strengthened my listening. Authenticity at home made me more genuine at work.

This isn't about oversharing or being unprofessional. It's about integrating emotional intelligence into every space you lead, creating coherence between who you are personally and professionally.

I had to unlearn the belief that leaders can't be vulnerable. I had to dismantle the idea that boundaries make me less available. What I found instead was that honesty makes me more grounded, more whole, and ultimately more effective.

High achievers don't avoid stress by being superhuman. They thrive because they develop the emotional intelligence and resilience to process adversity without losing their center. The more you understand your emotional landscape, the more resilient you become. And the more resilient you are, the more capacity you have for connection. Emotionally intelligent individuals overcome setbacks because they are equipped with the mental tools to do so.

Check-In Moment: Your Relationship Competence Mirror

Professional Relationship Strengths:

- What relational skills serve you well in work settings?

Personal Relationship Growth Areas:

- Which professional strengths become barriers in personal relationships?
- Where do you struggle to translate competence into intimacy?

Integration Opportunities:

- How might personal growth improve your professional leadership?
- What would change if you brought more authenticity into your work relationships?

Remember: You don't have to choose between competence and vulnerability.

The most effective leaders are both skilled and authentic, capable and human.

You don't have to perform closeness. You don't have to be strong in every conversation. You don't need to shrink your emotions to keep your seat at the table.

Your emotional self is not a liability. It's your compass.

And if you're going to navigate transitions with clarity, you need to let that compass guide you, especially when the map doesn't make sense.

This is where leadership gets real. This is how high achievers grow in relationships without losing themselves in the process.

Chapter Six

The *P.I.V.O.T* You Didn't Plan For

We move through life with surprisingly few moments of true contemplation, those rare pauses that make us question everything. From the beginning, we're handed ideas: how the world works, what's right and wrong, who we should become, what paths are worthy. Our parents offered what they knew, shaped by their own limits. But much of what guides us isn't chosen; it's absorbed, accumulated, and left unquestioned.

Other times, something cracks us open, whether it's a diagnosis, a loss, or a tragedy, and suddenly we see with unsettling clarity. *Life is short. Life is unpredictable.* You look back and wonder: *Why did I waste so much time? Why did I chase approval instead of peace?* The pivot feels forced, uninvited, and yet impossible to ignore.

At first, this awakening ignites a fire. You overhaul routines, break ties, or grasp at quick fixes that promise to fill the void. But soon the fire fades, and you're left circling: dread, hope, action, collapse. The same loop, played on repeat.

This book isn't about hype or temporary highs. It's about facing the pivot you never planned for.

The Vitality of An Overhaul

Real change doesn't start with vision boards or grand declarations. It starts with silence, the kind that forces you to hear your own truth. I had to strip away the noise: the comparisons, the endless proving, the addiction to "busy." My real work wasn't about chasing more; it was about releasing what was never mine.

To get to the good, we must first name the bad. Drag the shadows into light. The fears, the desires, the beliefs that cling to us like parasites. You can't conquer what you refuse to name. Overhauls are not about reinventing yourself into someone "better." They're about remembering the wholeness you buried under expectations.

The Death of the Old Me

There's no pivot without grief. Before you rise, something in you must die: the version that hustled for worth, the voice that said yes when my soul screamed no, the mask of perfection.

Here's the truth: your body renews itself every seven years. Dead cells replaced, old matter shed. Why should your identity be any different? Growth demands release. You are not your ego. Not your doubts, your fears, or your insecurities. You are the consciousness from which they arise. Like ripples on water, they pass. They do not define the ocean. In this section, you will learn how to shed the layers of ego, one limiting belief at a time.

The hardest funerals are the ones you hold for yourself. But in burying the old me, I gave permission for something new to breathe.

Of course, the mind resists. *Is it true?* it asks. *Can you really change? Or are you destined to perform forever, chasing approval, pretending at fulfillment?* That's the voice of the ego. But the ego is not the truth; it is only one lens, loud but limited.

Freud described the ego as the mind's referee, balancing instinct with reason. Useful, yes. But what he didn't say is that the ego also manipulates, judges, and suffocates the higher self. It hijacks perspective, confusing control with safety. The ego can keep you alive, but if left unchecked, it keeps you small.

But you are not your thoughts. Just because your ego-mind says something, it does not make it true. You're not your ego-mind, you're not the doubts and fears and anxieties. You're not the numbness, you're not the limiting beliefs, you're not a victim of your surroundings, of circumstances, of society, or of the world. Detach yourself from your ego, from its perversities and caprices, from its violent mood swings and irrational fits. Only when you do so will you be able to identify which thoughts should be ignored and discarded and which thoughts should be developed and nurtured.

Perspective is everything. Your ego sees the world from its own, often very limited perspective, and so its understanding of the world is deeply rooted in that limitation. Imagine walking into a house for the first time. Some notice the torn wallpaper, others the smell of cooking, others the arrangement of the furniture. Ten people, ten interpretations—all true, none complete. Reality works the same way. What you focus on shapes your experience of the world.

Everything that occurs in that reality is up for interpretation based on who you are, what you value, how you see the world, and so on. Your reality is filtered through what you perceive, much like it is for others and what they perceive. So, what makes the distinction between your reality and that of other people around you? The answer is your focus.

When you change your focus, you can change your perception, your reality, and by extension, your life. When you focus on your stress, it multiplies. When you focus on your fear, it expands. In that way, whatever you put your focus on becomes your perceived reality. So when you worry about all the problems you have and how impossible they seem, you're directing your mind toward all the negative repercussions that problem has on your life. This puts your focus on the obstacle itself and what it entails, but not the solution.

However, when you shift your focus, your subjective reality shifts with it, and your circumstances do too, as they move to represent that shift in perspective. This is the death of the old you: learning not to mistake the ripples for the ocean, not to mistake the ego for the self.

And when the ego loosens its grip, something becomes clear: the armor you've built may no longer fit. That's where the next step begins.

When the Life You Built No Longer Fits

At times, it may feel like you're a passive participant in your own life, an outsider, an onlooker, waiting for alignment to happen. Perhaps you've neglected your inner self so often that you no longer know what you truly want. You might even wonder if pursuing anything new is worth the effort, having grown accustomed to the comfort of your own protective bubble, clinging to the knowledge you've gathered about the world as if it were enough. But you don't have to keep enduring this emptiness just because you feel lost in how to navigate by the light of your own authenticity.

You are not destined to remain passive. You don't have to sit back and react to whatever life throws your way. You don't have to remain dissatisfied with who you've been. You can choose to be the protagonist of your own journey, to reclaim your passions instead of setting them aside for what seems "more important."

Reclaiming your life happens one step at a time. Too often, we get impatient with ourselves, giving only a limited number of chances before retreating into defeat. But there is always room—room for growth, room for healing, room for meaningful change.

And here's the truth: change doesn't demand erasing your identity or becoming someone entirely new. Real change is about healing, about investing in the courage to live more fully as yourself. But to take that step, you'll have to face the one barrier most people spend their whole lives avoiding: the fear of truly living.

Which Tense Are You Living In?

When we look back over our lives, we often realize how easily we've taken its beauty for granted. We tell ourselves there will be time later, time to slow down, to appreciate, to breathe. But then the years slip away like water through cupped hands. Five years. Ten years. Decades. And suddenly we're left wondering what has been lost, and if it's too late to realign with what matters most.

Some of us live stuck in the past, defined by pain or nostalgia. We replay old scenes, hoping they'll change if we study them long enough. Others sprint toward the future, convinced joy will appear at the next milestone, the next promotion, the next success. But here's the truth I had to learn: neither tense can hold you.

The past is a teacher, not a home. The future is a vision, not a guarantee. The present is the only place where healing happens, where alignment takes root. It's here, not back then and not out there, that we learn to remember, to accept, to let go, and to trust the journey.

This is about reclaiming that chance, about reinventing yourself so that you are proud of who you are, what you do, and how you do it. Because we only get one life, no take-backs, no redos. And if you're holding this book, I know something inside you is already stirring: maybe a quiet awareness that success on paper hasn't translated into fulfillment, maybe a longing to feel alive again, or maybe a desire to reclaim the parts of yourself buried beneath roles, routines, and expectations.

Wherever you find yourself, the progression forward is the same: to remember, to accept, to let go, and to trust the journey. Not by rushing into the future or clinging to the past, but by choosing to live fully here.

Get Over Your Fear of Life

The best and perhaps only approach to fully understand where you are and whether you are ready for change is the practice of mindfulness. Not the trendy version we scroll past on social media, but the raw practice of staying present, even when life feels unbearable. It takes endurance to sit with yourself without numbing, distracting, or running. But presence is where insight, clarity, and healing begin. And to step into that space, you first have to get over your fear of life.

We assume death is the enemy, but most of us are far more afraid of living. Afraid of opening our hearts. Afraid of pursuing what we love. Afraid of being fully seen. Vulnerability feels like danger, so we build walls and call them protection. We worship busyness, idolize composure, and convince ourselves that restraint is strength. We bury our emotions under performance, telling ourselves it's maturity.

But deep down, we know the truth: we've betrayed ourselves. We've traded feeling for achievement, authenticity for approval, presence for productivity. That betrayal, not failure in the workplace or disappointment in relationships, is the deepest wound we carry.

I had to face that in myself, to admit that no accolade could fill the emptiness that came from ignoring my own heart. The world tells us to do more, feel less, but it's a lie. Real living requires the opposite. It asks us to walk straight into our fear of pain, of failure, of joy, of love, and to trust that what's on the other side is worth it.

Here's the hard part: no book, no workshop, no quick inspiration can do it for you. Change isn't about consuming more information. It's about daring to sit in the silence after the last page is turned, when the motivation fades and the fear creeps back in, and choosing differently this time.

Every ounce of reason we possess prevents us from experiencing the full intensity of our emotions, and by extension, life. And because we're so afraid of raw emotions, of the unrefined taste of life, we seek control, power, and mastery over ourselves as well as over our surroundings.

We admire cool, calm, and collected people—those who don't show their emotions, those who calculate and anticipate, those who never falter in their step. We idolize unshakable confidence, we revere discipline, we worship restraint. Surely, successful people got to where they are by self-restraint and continence. Surely, they rose above their vulnerability and compulsion. Surely, they detached themselves from the feeble human shell to transcend as superior beings. I did, and I am quite certain you did too.

We're convinced that the modern individual's entire worth resides in how committed they are to being successful, more so than being a person. And thus, we all try to belong to this action-based and result-driven generation with an infallible motto: feel less and do more. So, regardless of how we perform in our personal and professional lives, we will always be a failure as a person.

This isn't meant to discourage you or minimize the successes you've achieved. On the contrary, it's meant to push you to acknowledge that sense of failure within yourself so you can overcome your fear of living. Because it is a failure, after all. We have failed ourselves miserably, betrayed ourselves in a way that success alone cannot mend.

This is why self-help and self-improvement books are so popular, but it's also why they fail to make us change permanently. We fall back into old habits, first disappointed, then angry that we allowed ourselves to dream for a moment, our thoughts a scrambled blur of guilt, shame, and confusion: *Did you really believe this was it, your golden ticket to a new personality and a different life? How naive.*

But here's the truth: the book was never the ticket. **You are.** The words may fade, but your choice to face the fear of life, to sit with your raw emotions, to feel instead of flee, to live instead of perform— that is what creates lasting change.

The Art of Being

Achievement is addictive. There's always another finish line, another task, another proving ground. But healing forced me to learn the art of being. I had to unlearn the compulsion to always do.

For me, "being" meant sitting with my feelings instead of fixing them. It meant journaling until the words poured out raw, meditating on silence, and allowing myself to exist without needing a title or task to justify my presence. It felt awkward at first, like walking without armor, but it became the soil where wholeness could finally take root.

Modern life rarely makes space for this. We are constantly drained because one part of us is always at war with another: the ego striving for control, the rational mind suppressing the heart, the spirit trying to outrun fear. That inner conflict exhausts us more than any workload ever could.

While this, in large part, occurs in our unconscious mind, its effects manifest on a more perceivable level, one that exhausts our energy and ravages our peace of mind. So we try to run as far away as possible from these festering thoughts. We occupy ourselves, we engage in monotonous conversations and brainless activities, all to avoid the monstrous clasp of our brains. But we fail to recognize that tiny voice in our heads that keeps telling us we are not enough.

But when you stop running, when you choose to simply be, you discover something radical: pain does not destroy you. Avoidance does. Sitting with your truth opens the doorway to acceptance, and acceptance is where joy begins.

This Pivot Wasn't in My Planner

I'm a strategist by nature. I like to know the plan, map the steps, anticipate the outcomes.

But when life called me to evolve, when cancer hit, when the grief caught up to me, when the uniform came off at night, I didn't have a roadmap. What I had was a choice:

Keep pretending I was still that old version of myself, or start building the life I actually needed now.

So I pivoted.

Not overnight.

Not perfectly.

But intentionally.

I started listening more.

Slowing down.

Creating space to hear my own voice, outside of the noise, the roles, the expectations.

And what I found was real change doesn't come from wrestling one part of yourself into submission. You can't fight your ego with willpower and expect peace. That only deepens the conflict. Transformation requires kindness, compassion, and self-acceptance, not a civil war within.

When life threw me into uncharted territory, my first instinct was to resist. That's what we do as humans: cling to the familiar, avoid the discomfort, choose flight over fight. But growth lives in the unfamiliar. It asks us to notice how our inner condition shapes the way we meet external challenges.

We are creatures of habit, conditioned by routines, environments, and expectations. But habits alone don't define destiny. What does is the set of beliefs we choose to carry forward, the ones that shape how we see ourselves and the world. To truly change, we must release beliefs that no longer serve us, even when it feels like ripping out roots.

So I had to pause and ask myself:

- What season of life am I actually in?
- What is it teaching me?
- What am I holding onto that limits me?
- Am I chasing someone else's definition of success — or my own?
- What fears am I letting dictate my decisions?
- If I don't shift now, where will I be in a year?

These weren't questions I could rush through. They unsettled me. They forced me to acknowledge both gratitude and grief, to see that the same challenges that broke me also became the soil of my purpose.

Here's the truth: pivots are rarely planned. They arrive disguised as interruptions, heartbreaks, or closed doors. But when you stop resisting and start listening, you find that what felt like disruption was actually direction.

So, I'll leave you with this: *If not now, when? If not you, then who? And if not this life, what other chance do you think you'll get?*

Check-In Moment: What Are You Holding That's Holding You Back?

Let's take a pause. Breathe deep. Be honest.

- What part of your identity no longer feels true, but you're still performing it?

- Where have you outgrown your own life, but feel guilty for saying so?

- What would you release today if you trusted that something better was waiting on the other side?

You don't have to burn everything down. But you do have to stop pretending that nothing needs to change.

Reinvention doesn't mean you failed. It means you're brave enough to evolve.

And this pivot, this quiet awakening in your spirit—It's not a detour. It's a divine invitation to become who you were always meant to be.

Let's keep moving.

Chapter Seven

A.I.M. – Acknowledge, Identify, Move

For years, I equated forward motion with success. If I kept producing, kept achieving, kept pressing ahead, I believed fulfillment would eventually catch up. But I had to face the truth: forward motion without reflection only creates burnout. The A.I.M. Method—Acknowledge, Identify, Move—was born out of my own need to slow down, listen inward, and reset before moving again with clarity. I knew I had to create something that felt human, something that allowed me to navigate the confusion rediscovering entails.

I needed a quick and simple method that could hold both my professional competence and my personal vulnerability, something that honored where I had been while creating space for who I was becoming.

The A.I.M. Method emerged not from theory but from necessity. It became my practical roadmap for moving through uncharted territory, between who I had been trained to be and who I was discovering myself to be. It's not just another shiny self-help method that promises you the world and delivers little more than existential vapor. This was my lifeline, and I am handing it to you, to the version of you that is ready to lead themselves and others from a place of love, integrity, and authenticity.

A- ACKNOWLEDGE

Acknowledgement isn't about weakness—it's about honesty. You can't reset if you won't recognize where you are.

There are three levels of acknowledgement:

1. **Surface Awareness:** noticing stress, fatigue, or the fact that things just don't feel right.

2. **Pattern Recognition:** realizing the recurring habits of overcommitment, comparison, and avoidance that keep showing up.

   - "I've built my identity around being needed"

   - "I don't know who I am without my title"

   - "I'm afraid to slow down because I might become irrelevant"

   - "I've been performing competence while feeling internally lost"

3. **Foundational Truth:** naming what's really underneath. Sometimes it's grief. Sometimes fear. Sometimes a quiet voice saying, *"This is not who I am anymore."* This is the deepest level: acknowledging the structural gaps in our preparation for this transition.

   - "My education prepared me to solve everyone's problems except my own"

- "I've become an expert at external management but a novice at internal navigation"

- "I'm professionally successful but personally unprepared for this level of change"

While we all tend to warp reality in one way or another, whether through our perspectives, beliefs, or opinions, the subconscious production of these stories can influence the way we view ourselves, other people, and the world around us. Sometimes this is simply the result of our unconscious values and experiences, but other times it's more conscious and deliberate, an attempt to distort what is factual as a way of avoiding hard realities we'd rather not acknowledge.

The stories we create are the very reason behind our suffering. When we sculpt our own construct of the nature of the world, we also set expectations of that world, and when those expectations go unmet, they lead to resistance, anguish, and torment. Some of our personal beliefs stem from experiences we've had, often overgeneralizations of how life is supposed to be lived.

Marcus Aurelius once said, *"The soul becomes dyed with the color of its thoughts."* Our minds dictate how our days unfold; they shape our entire human experience, much like the lens of a camera determines the quality of its pictures. A defective lens will produce poor images, and a mind saturated with limiting beliefs and negative voices will produce a life of discomfort and inadequacy.

You can't heal what you refuse to name. And when you finally do, you often discover the weight you've been carrying wasn't the title, the task list, or the expectations—it was the silence around what you wouldn't admit.

My Acknowledgment Journey

The beliefs you hold ultimately shape the focus of your life. Mental dust, those old assumptions and unchecked habits, tarnishes judgment and clouds clarity. When life pressed pause for me, the phrase *"life is short"* took on a sharper, undeniable meaning.

When I first received my diagnosis, my acknowledgments unfolded in layers:

- **Surface:** *"This is a health challenge I need to manage and prepare for mentally."*

- **Pattern:** *"I've been treating my body like a machine, expecting it to obey without question."*

- **Foundational:** *"All my training didn't prepare me to lead myself through my own grief."*

The foundational acknowledgment was the hardest, because it meant admitting that expertise had limits, and no title, credential, or bank account could shield me from being fully human. My turning point came when I acknowledged more than just the diagnosis: my burnout, my unspoken grief, and the reality that my titles no longer fulfilled me.

That's where healing truly began, not with action alone but with truth.

But acknowledgment alone wasn't enough. Truth cracks the armor, but clarity builds the path. I needed to know who I was beneath the roles, titles, and expectations I had worn for years. That search for clarity led me into the next stage: Identify.

I- IDENTIFY

Identify is about excavation. It's the peeling back of professional layers, conditioned habits, and survival patterns to discover the operating system underneath. It's not about reinventing yourself but uncovering what's already been there, hidden under years of achievement or survival.

For me, that excavation meant stripping away the layers—soldier, leader, achiever—and finding the quiet dreamer, the writer, the woman who longed for health and wholeness on her own terms. That discovery didn't happen overnight. It took journaling, prayer, and honest conversations with myself about what mattered most beyond titles and responsibilities.

We rarely think about our true purpose in life. Like most people, we follow the path that seems the most convenient or materially rewarding at the time. This usually happens to be the safest path as well. We're taught not to take big risks because we might not bounce back from failure. Instead, we wander around aimlessly, chasing things that don't matter. Sometimes these things bring us temporary relief. Other times, they only bring us pain and a deep sense of discontent.

Identity is not static. It evolves. And when you identify who you are in this season, not who you were ten years ago, you unlock permission to live aligned, not just accomplished. Transitions will always test identity, and if it's tied only to titles or outcomes, you'll unravel when those things shift.

My Identify Journey

When my professional identity began to crack, I realized I had built so much of my worth on what I did rather than who I was. The Army had given me titles, credentials, and recognition, but when the noise quieted, I had to ask: *Who am I without all of this?*

For years, I had confused my capabilities with my essence. I thought accomplishment was proof of worth. But healing required me to separate the two. My degrees, ranks, and certifications were valid, but they were expressions of my abilities, not the definition of me.

One practice that helped was introducing myself without a résumé attached. Stripping away job titles, achievements, and affiliations forced me to sit with the question: *Who is Jada when the armor of accomplishment is gone?* At first, it felt like standing exposed, but it was also freeing.

Professional Identity Integration

This reflection showed me I was running on two operating systems:

- **Professional Operating System (learned through training):** achievement-driven, results-focused, fueled by external validation.

- **Personal Operating System (authentic tendencies):** rooted in connection, creativity, peace, growth.

They weren't enemies; they coexisted. The problem was that I had been feeding one while starving the other. That imbalance led me to what I now call Values **Archaeology**: digging beneath the values my profession rewarded (competition, efficiency, control) to rediscover the ones that truly sustained me (purpose, authenticity, relationships, integrity).

The challenge became clear: *How could I honor both worlds without betraying either one?*

My Identity Excavation Process

Frameworks are useful, but the real excavation began with deeper questions:

- What do I enjoy when no one is watching?

- What conversations am I hungry to have?

- What energizes me, and what drains me?

- What parts of myself have I put aside to maintain my professional image?

The answers surprised me. Beneath the polished image of titles and responsibility, I found I was hungry for creative expression, deep conversation, wholesome relationships, and unstructured time. None of these had been priorities in my achievement-focused life, yet they were essential to my wholeness.

This excavation wasn't about abandoning the professional side of me; it was about reclaiming the personal side I had buried.

M- MOVE

Acknowledgement without movement leads to stagnation. Identity without action remains theory. Movement is where integration happens.

Movement happens in phases:

1. **Micro-Moves:** small, consistent steps—choosing rest without guilt, setting one boundary, or saying no when everything in you wants to default to yes.

    o *Professional Application:* A cyber leader might simply block one hour for reflection each week rather than packing the schedule wall to wall.

2. **Aligned Action:** beginning to build systems, habits, and rhythms that reflect your true self instead of your survival mode.

    o *Professional Application:* creating space in team meetings for lessons learned, not just polished wins.

3. **Embodied Living:** when your choices, your calendar, and your relationships all align with who you truly are. Movement feels less like striving and more like breathing.

   o *Professional Application:* leading not from urgency, but from presence and clarity—modeling what it means to operate regulated, not reactive.

A great tragedy is that most people never work on materializing their ideas out of fear of failure or judgment, or lack of time, or some other paltry excuse. They keep waiting for the right moment and the right time, but life happens, and their ideas never come to fruition.

One of the greatest sayings about doing something right now and not later or tomorrow comes from Les Brown:

"The graveyard is the richest place on earth because it is here that you will find all the hopes and dreams that were never fulfilled, the books that were never written, the songs that were never sung, the inventions that were never shared, the cures that were never discovered, all because someone was too afraid to take that first step, keep with the problem, or determined to carry out their dream."

Taking action is everything that matters to you right now, and everything that stands between you and taking action is simply the first step. Dreams can come true, but dreams require action after you transmute your desire into a goal backed by a plan. After all, talk is cheap, so do you have what it takes to take action right now?

Remember: movement doesn't have to be massive to be meaningful. Micro-moves compound. Aligned action stacks. Over time, they create a new normal that reflects your true identity.

"The impediment to action advances action. What stands in the way becomes the way."—Marcus Aurelius, *Meditations*

My Movement Journey

My movement through recovery and healing happened in the phases"

Phase 1 – Internal Work

I focused on the unseen first: therapy, journaling, detoxing from distractions, and learning to sit with my truth instead of trying to fix it immediately. I had to build the muscle of honesty before I could move with integrity.

Phase 2 – Shared Vulnerability

Once I could hold my own truth, I began sharing pieces of my journey with trusted people. That vulnerability carried into my leadership style, where I no longer pretended to have all the answers but created space for authenticity in myself and others.

Phase 3 – Rebuilding from the Inside Out

Eventually, my entire approach to leadership shifted. I no longer measured strength by how much I could endure silently but by how much I could lead with alignment. This phase became the foundation of my practice, helping other professionals navigate their own transitions without losing themselves.

The Professional Boundaries Reset

Movement also required resetting boundaries, shifting from survival-driven patterns to sustainable wholeness.

Old Model: External expectations drive everything

- "I should be available whenever needed."
- "I can't say no to career opportunities."
- "Personal needs are secondary to professional demands."
- "I must maintain perfection at all times."

New Model: Sustainable wholeness enables better performance

- "I respond to needs within my capacity for sustainable excellence."
- "I choose opportunities that align with my authentic development."
- "Personal well-being enables my best professional contribution."
- "I lead from love, integrity, and authenticity—including acknowledging when I'm still learning."

Check-In Moment: Where Are You in the A.I.M. Process?

Before moving forward, pause and locate yourself in this journey:

- **Acknowledge** – What's the truth I've been avoiding?

- **Identify** – Who am I beyond my roles, and what do I need in this season?

- **Move** – What is one small, aligned action I can take this week to support my wholeness?

Remember: **A.I.M. isn't a one-time process.** It's a lifelong practice of staying connected to your whole self while navigating the demands of life and work.

You don't need to have it all figured out.

You just need to take the next aligned step.

You've spent years aiming for excellence.

Now it's time to **A.I.M. for wholeness.**

You're not behind.

You are right on time.

The next chapter isn't waiting out there—it's already in you.

This is how you move from external success to integrated significance.

Chapter Eight

The Inner Game of Reinvention

For years, I ran on pure adrenaline and unbridled ambition. I had the degrees, the credentials, and the structure. I certainly knew how to get things done, even when I didn't feel like it. What I failed to realize, however, was that my momentum was coming from pressure, not peace. I thought mindset work was something other people needed, people who lacked discipline, education, or proper training. The idea that I needed to examine my thought patterns seemed unnecessary when I had such obvious evidence of my mental effectiveness.

I was wrong.

As a high achiever navigating major life changes, I discovered that the mental frameworks that got me to where I was couldn't take me where I needed to go. I needed a practical reset, not of my capabilities, but of the internal operating system driving them. If you're simply gritting your teeth and pushing through, that's a dangerous thing. You can fool everyone, at times even yourself, into thinking it's working, until your internal world starts to collapse. This is when you learn that real leadership work starts in the mind, from within.

The High Achiever's Mindset Paradox

Accomplished professionals face a unique challenge in reinvention: the very mental patterns that created our success often become the barriers to our evolution. We're not starting with a broken mindset that needs fixing; we're working with a highly effective mindset that needs updating. Your mindset influences every aspect of your life. It governs your perception of your creativity, intelligence, effectiveness, skills, and even well-being.

The Success-Trap Mindset Patterns

Pattern 1: Worth=Output *The Achievement Equation*

- We got you here: "I am valuable when I produce valuable results"

- Why it worked: Created drive, focus, and measurable success

- Why it fails in transition: You can't "produce" your way through identity evolution

- The reset: "I am inherently valuable and express that value through meaningful contribution"

Pattern 2: Control=Safety *The Certainty Addiction*

- What got you here: "If I plan thoroughly and execute precisely, I can control outcomes"

- Why it worked: Created professional competence and reliable results

- Why it fails in transition: Personal transformation requires embracing uncertainty

- The reset: "I find safety in my ability to respond wisely to whatever emerges"

Pattern 3: Expertise=Identity *The Credential Trap*

- What got you here: "I am what I know and what I can do"

- Why it worked: Built confidence and professional reputation

- Why it fails in transition: You become afraid to be a beginner at anything

- The reset: "My expertise is a tool I use, not who I am

Pattern 4: Perfect=Acceptable *The Excellence Prison*

- What got you here: *"Anything less than exceptional performance is failure"*

- Why it worked: *Created high standards and impressive results*

- Why it fails in transition: *Evolution requires experimenting, which means inevitable imperfection*

- The reset: *"Progress and learning are more valuable than perfect performance"*

The Practical Mindset Reset for Change Navigation

Reset #1: From Performance Identity to Integrated Identity

Old Operating System: "I am successful, therefore I am valuable"

Updated Operating System: "I am valuable and express that value through both being and doing"

Practical Implementation:

- **Morning Practice:** Start each day by asking "Who am I choosing to be today?" before "What do I need to accomplish?"

- **Decision Filter:** Before major choices, ask "Does this align with who I'm becoming, not just what I've been?"

- **Success Redefinition:** Measure progress by alignment and growth, not just achievement and recognition

Reset #2: From Control Orientation to Response Orientation

Old Operating System: "I must control outcomes to feel safe"

Updated Operating System: "I build resilience through my capacity to respond skillfully to any outcome"

Practical Implementation:

- **Weekly Planning:** Plan your responses and preparation, but hold outcomes lightly

- **Uncertainty Practice:** Each week, do something small with an unknown outcome

- **Response Repertoire:** Develop multiple ways to respond to setbacks instead of trying to prevent all setbacks

Reset #3: From Fixed Expertise to Growth Expertise

Old Operating System: "I must maintain my expert status at all costs"

Updated Operating System: "My expertise gives me confidence to learn and grow in new areas"

Practical Implementation:

- **Learning Projects:** Regularly engage in activities where you're a beginner

- **Curiosity Practice:** Ask more questions in areas where you're supposed to be the expert

- **Knowledge Integration:** Connect your expertise to new interests rather than defending its boundaries

Reset #4: From Perfection Standards to Evolution Standards

Old Operating System: "If it's not excellent, it shouldn't be attempted"

Updated Operating System: "Done with learning is better than perfect but stagnant"

Practical Implementation:

- **Iteration Mindset:** Approach changes as experiments you can adjust rather than permanent decisions you must get right

- **Progress Tracking:** Measure how much you're growing, not just how well you're performing

- **Failure Reframing:** View setbacks as data for your next iteration rather than evidence of inadequacy

The High Achiever's Thought Pattern Audit

Identifying Limiting Patterns That Masquerade as Strengths

The Overcommitment Pattern

- **Surface thought:** "I'm dedicated and reliable"

- **Deeper pattern:** "I'm only valuable when I'm indispensable"

- **Reset:** "I serve best when I serve sustainably"

The Independence Pattern

- **Surface thought:** "I'm self-sufficient and capable"

- **Deeper pattern:** "Asking for help reveals weakness"

- **Reset:** "Collaboration enhances rather than threatens my competence"

The Analysis Paralysis Pattern

- **Surface thought:** "I'm thorough and strategic"

- **Deeper pattern:** "I must have certainty before I can act"

- **Reset:** "I gather wisdom and then act with courage"

The Comparison Pattern

- **Surface thought:** "I'm competitive and driven"

- **Deeper pattern:** "Others' success diminishes my worth"

- **Reset:** "Others' success inspires possibilities for my own growth"

The Integration Challenge: Living Your Reset

The goal isn't to abandon the mental patterns that created your success; it's to update them for your next level of growth. You keep the drive but evolve the direction. You maintain the standards but expand the definition of success. You preserve the competence but integrate it with authenticity.

Your Personal Mindset Reset Plan

Step 1: Identify Your Primary Success Pattern Which of the four patterns (worth=output, control=safety, expertise=identity, perfect=acceptable) most defines your current approach?

Step 2: Design Your Specific Reset What would the updated version of this pattern look like for you personally and professionally?

Step 3: Create Implementation Systems What daily, weekly, and monthly practices will help you live from your updated mindset?

Step 4: Build Accountability Structures Who in your life can support your mindset evolution without judging your process?

Check-In Moment: Your Mindset Reality Check

- What mental pattern served you well in building your success but now limits your growth?

- Where are you afraid to change your thinking because it might threaten your achievements?

- What would be possible if you updated your internal operating system while keeping your external competencies?

Remember: You're not changing who you are—you're updating how you think about who you are. You're updating your:

- Relationship to success and failure

- Source of security and worth

- Approach to uncertainty and learning

- Definition of strength and competence

- Understanding of sustainable performance

The Result: You become more effective, not less. More authentic, not unprofessional. More resilient, not weaker.

This integration approach allows high achievers to evolve without losing the very qualities that made them successful in the first place.

The next chapter is calling.

Chapter Nine

Building a Framework for Resilience

Resilience is often romanticized as a heroic rebound, a phoenix rising from the ashes. But what's rarely examined is the cost of constantly having to rise. We seldom ask the harder, more sobering question: *Why must we keep recovering in the first place?*

I've lived resilience not as a badge of honor but as a survival strategy—weathering illness while remaining dutiful, mourning in silence while leading others, appearing composed while quietly unraveling. This isn't a sermon on grit; it's a reckoning with its limits.

Without a deliberate architecture for emotional sustainability, resilience becomes another mask we wear while quietly burning out. True strength isn't bouncing back; it's building a life that doesn't require you to break.

Resilience Is Not Just Bouncing Back—It's Building Well

Some challenges barely dent us; others change us so deeply we fear we'll never feel "normal" again. Days blur, hope flickers, and we silently punish ourselves for not being "strong enough." But that is *not resilience.*

Resilience doesn't mean suppressing your emotions or putting on a façade. It means finding strength through them, understanding where they come from, what they need, and how to work with them.

Resilience is deeply personal. It's not a fixed way to manage problems; it's subjective, and it varies from one person to the next. What fortifies me may not fortify you. But resilience becomes more sustainable when we focus on five essential capacities:

#Flexibility

People often mistake flexibility for self-denial. You can be adaptable while still allowing others the space to express themselves. Flexibility is the ability to adapt without abandoning your principles and values, to shift between optimism and pessimism so you see the whole picture.

We're always told to view life from a positive standpoint, that negativity and pessimism will only set us back. But pessimism is important sometimes. Using the inversion mindset, starting with the outcome you don't want, sharpens clarity, reveals hidden fears, and helps you design a realistic plan forward.

#Self-esteem

This is one of the most important aspects of resilience. Healthy self-esteem is self-awareness, self-acceptance, and self-respect, not an inflated ego or a polished façade. It also goes far beyond personality constructs. It's knowing your worth while honoring your boundaries. Without it, resilience rests on shaky ground.

This is a vital element of resilience because it encompasses the micro components that are absolutely necessary for us to build and nurture a healthy concept of the world and our place in it.

But because this is such a broad and expansive ideal, it also brings confusion and misconceptions. Some mistake healthy self-esteem for exuding a confident façade, while others associate it with a ruthless ability to reject or even hurt others without feeling guilty. This couldn't be further from the truth.

#Emotional control

True emotional control isn't suppression; it's recognition. It's channeling frustration, stress, or sadness into intentional action. It's slowing down before reacting and creating space for others to feel seen and safe.

Emotional control is denying yourself quick fixes and the temporary relief they bring because you know better than to succumb to instant gratification, and most importantly, because you're aware of how rewarding the outcome will be.

When you're more mindful of your emotions, whether they stem from fear or despair, you're less likely to be overwhelmed, especially when things don't go as planned, because you trust yourself and others to rise above the challenge, no matter how difficult it seems.

#Persistence

Persistence isn't blind optimism; it's the foundation of resilience. It's the commitment to keep going while staying realistic. It's knowing when to push forward, when to pause, and when to let go. Whether you're dealing with a setback or internal conflict, your determination to learn and grow will help you power through difficulties.

You know a lost cause when you see one. You recognize when to disengage in the face of insolvency, but you also trust your discernment to know when to keep going and press on. Knowing when to cut your losses is an essential quality that very few people have. It's equally as important as knowing when to stay the course and carry on. A key element to building resilience is sticking to your goals and resolutions, even when that pushes you to face your fears.

#Strong relationships

Resilience is easier when we're not carrying the load alone. Healthy connections expand our capacity to endure and adapt, and they challenge our blind spots if we let them.

Having strong interpersonal relationships is both a by-product and a prerequisite of resilience. If you have the power to build and maintain healthy personal bonds with others, both at work and outside of work, then you have already taken the first step toward a resilient life.

We are social creatures by nature, even the most introverted of us, and being around others gives us the strength to endure difficult times, overcome our problems, and evolve from them. The experience of cultivating and nurturing strong relationships changes you at the deepest levels; it shapes the way you see the world and how you view yourself.

So to build resilience, we first need to develop our capacity to strengthen our interpersonal relationships and open ourselves to new ones. As a result, our emotional intelligence sharpens, and so do our coping mechanisms.

Although we tend to think of ourselves as open-minded and nonjudgmental, sometimes we don't give other people the chance they deserve. Whether out of fear or self-preservation, we're quick to put them in a box, slap a label on it, and move on. While first impressions are important, they're not everything. No matter how different someone is from you, there's always something to learn, and there's always an opportunity for growth and personal development, though only if you allow it to manifest.

If you wish to be capable of rising to great challenges, you must first rise to everyday, ordinary challenges. You must stop making excuses for why you can't and begin cultivating the reasons and the responses for why you can.

Resilience is not reactive in that regard. It's proactive by nature, and it requires building a foundation strong enough to withstand challenges in the first place.

My Three Pillars of Resilience

For high-performers like us, for high-performers, toughness alone eventually cracks. That's why I built a framework I could actually live with—three pillars that keep me grounded and capable:

Pillar One: Emotional Safety – Stop Abandoning Yourself

Resilience starts with allowing your emotions to exist without judgment.

When you are mindful of your emotional experience, you can begin to uncover valuable insights into how your mind deals with stressful situations. It's about reframing the conversations you have within yourself and then transforming how you show up in the external world.

It is not about pushing through but about being fully present with your experience and honoring your feelings. The most important thing to understand is that you can boost your resilience because it's a cluster of adaptive behaviors.

Ask yourself:

- Am I creating space to feel without shame?

- Do I check in with my emotions before they erupt?

- Can I be honest with myself even when it's uncomfortable?

Tool: *The RAIN Method*

- **Recognize** what you're feeling- meaning to consciously acknowledge the thoughts, feelings, and behaviors that are affecting you. Name your emotions.

- **Allow** it to be there- Allowing creates space to make wise decisions.

- **Investigate** with grace- meaning calling on your curiosity and directing your attention to your present experience.

- **Non-identify-** you are not your emotions. Meaning, loosen your sense of who you think you are and create more expansiveness around your sense of self. Emotions come and go like the weather, but who you are remains steady underneath.

Pillar Two: Energetic Boundaries – Protect What Can't Be Replaced

Your time, energy, and focus are limited. Boundaries keep them from being consumed by urgency and noise.

Steps to set and keep them:

1. **Identify priorities** — Know what truly matters.

2. **Spot patterns** — Notice behaviors, both yours and others', that erode your capacity. We often focus on remedying the roadblocks rather than the patterns that cause them. Eliminate the root of the problem.

3. **Hold the line** — Communicate boundaries clearly and reinforce them consistently. Most of the time, these boundary violations are unintentional. Not everyone will be aware of your boundaries unless you explain them, and even then, they might forget or fall back into their habits.

Pillar Three: Intentional Recovery – Don't Just Power Down, Reconnect

Recovery isn't collapsing on the couch or on your bed; it's actively refueling your mind, body, and spirit.

We wear so many hats to fulfill all the roles and responsibilities we're entrusted with. Yet we cannot remember which, if any, of those hats solely belong to us. Some characteristics we've been assigned, some we've had to develop, yet none are an entire and accurate representation of our unique selves. We have lost ourselves in the process.

So, how do we restore what has been lost? How do we find a healthy equilibrium that allows us to be ourselves, flaws and all, while maintaining control and self-organization?

For me, that looked like:

- Self-acceptance

- Journaling or making notes in my phone after hard conversations.

- Drinking water before caffeine or tea.

- Walking without a podcast.

- Laughing—on purpose.

- Letting people love me without earning it.

With compassion and kindness, you can rebuild trust with yourself and teach your body that it's safe to stop running.

Check-In Moment: Build Your Framework

You don't need a crisis to start structuring resilience.

Ask yourself:

- What does emotional safety look like in my daily life?

- Where do I need stronger energetic boundaries?

- What are three recovery practices I can do weekly—not just in emergencies?

Write it. Live it. Adjust as you grow.

Because the truth is, your capacity will expand in proportion to your structure.

And you don't need to break down to rebuild.

You can choose now to create a life that's not just successful—but sustainable.

Chapter Ten

From Success to Significance

I knew how to win. I had chased the goals, collected the milestones, and worn the armor of accomplishment so well that no one could see the cracks. Yet I couldn't help but feel a sense of disconnect, a quiet unrest tugging at me, a knowing that this couldn't be all there was. It pervaded everything I did. It wasn't fatigue or failure. This went much deeper. That subtle but irrepressible knowing made me realize that what once brought fulfillment had become just another meaningless performance.

In that stillness, it became clear to me that external success was never the pinnacle. I was wrong to believe that my true calling was achievement. It was actually significance.

The Danger of Success as Identity

When you've worked relentlessly to excel, success becomes sacred. It mistakenly becomes your identity. It validates the sleepless nights, the sacrifices, the invisible battles. It whispers, *You made it. You are enough.*

But what happens when the applause fades and your soul feels unmoved? That's when success reveals its shadow: an emptiness dressed in accomplishment. What you feel isn't failure; it's dissonance. And that's often the first signal you're evolving.

I remember sitting in a room where my presence commanded respect, yet internally, I had already left. I hadn't outgrown my capacity; I had outgrown the context.

When what once defined you no longer reflects you, success becomes a cage.

The Conditioning That Keeps Us There

From an early age, many of us were taught that feelings are liabilities. To see vulnerability as weakness. To compete, not connect. We were encouraged to harden, to guard ourselves, to play it safe.

We hear *no* more often than yes, until it becomes our default setting, even against ourselves. We trade our inner truth for external validation, hoping it will fill the void. But validation fades. And without alignment, even the biggest wins feel small.

So we build fortresses around our hearts and perform the roles expected of us. We strive, we achieve, we prove, but underneath, fear quietly drives the show. And because of that fear, we cling to external validation like oxygen. It soothes for a moment but never heals the wound that whispers, *"You still aren't enough."*

What Is Significance, Really?

Significance is depth over display. It is not the pursuit of recognition, but the embodiment of purpose. It's not about being known; it's about leaving a mark that outlives the moment.

I began to understand significance not in the spotlight, but in the shadows of real conversations: mentoring someone through doubt, guiding a team member who felt unseen, or sharing a piece of my own pain that gave them permission to exhale.

True significance does not beckon attention; it leaves a residue long after the moment is over. It's the kind of impact that doesn't require your name to be remembered, because the change you created still lives on in someone else.

The Courage to Evolve, Even When You're Winning

Evolving when you're losing is expected. Evolving while you're still "winning" is terrifying. That's courage.

It means releasing the safety of what you know. It means forgiving the past, embracing imperfection, and trading performance for presence. It means recognizing you've always been enough, not because of what you've achieved, but because of who you are.

For me, that moment came after my cancer diagnosis. I didn't follow the traditional path of treatment. Instead, I trusted myself. I chose surgery, and then I chose to heal holistically. No chemo. No radiation. I leaned on faith, natural medicine, and my body's ability to regenerate. That choice wasn't just about health; it was about reclaiming authorship of my own life.

That choice required a different kind of faith, one that taught me resilience isn't just physical or about bouncing back quickly or hiding the scars. It's spiritual and mental too. I learned that just as the body needs integration to fully heal, leadership requires wholeness to truly endure. Nothing strips away illusions of control like facing your own fragility.

In that season, I realized something life-changing: success could never save me. Titles, promotions, and performance evaluations couldn't touch the battles I was fighting internally. What did save me was learning to trust myself, choosing to honor my body, and recognizing that leadership, like healing, isn't about perfection, but about presence.

That realization gave me permission to forgive myself for the years I let fear steer my choices. It taught me to embrace insecurities instead of hiding them and to replace self-criticism with self-compassion.

True courage is not stacking achievements but surrendering to your own wholeness. It's releasing the illusion that you have to do more to be enough. Fear will always push you to prove, but fulfillment invites you to be.

Check-In Moment: Are You Ready for More?

Let's pause.

- Where has success become a substitute for purpose?

- What are you afraid to walk away from because of what people might say?

- If you stopped striving and started living for impact, what would shift?

Success was never the end goal. You were always built for significance.

Now that you know who you are.

Now that you've acknowledged, identified, and realigned.

It's time to lead from that place.

Because someone's waiting for the version of you that's free.

Chapter Eleven

The Courage to Be Seen

Once, I mistook strength for seamless performance. I took great pride in my ability to remain composed, articulate, and unshaken amid chaos. For a time, this mastery of image earned me respect, even praise. But over time, I came to see that being celebrated for my steadfastness had made me invisible to myself.

The truth was, I wasn't leading from authenticity; I was curating a persona. I became a master of *strategic visibility*, knowing how to present my best self, highlight my strengths, and manage my professional image.

We can curate our competence so well that we lose touch with our own complexity. But there's a difference between being visible and being seen.

Being Visible: Others observe your performance, achievements, and professional persona

Being Seen: Others witness your humanity, growth, and authentic self

Earlier in this book, we explored how *identity drives behavior*, how the version of yourself you believe in most becomes the one you live out loud. For years, my visible self and my true self were at odds. My uniform, my credentials, my composed demeanor all created visibility while ensuring that no one, including myself, could truly see the person underneath.

The turning point came when I chose to abandon this obsession with performance and embrace something far more radical: vulnerability and truth as acts of self-recognition. This is where I stand now, and exactly where I'm leading you.

That moment marked my shift from leading with credentials to leading with authenticity, from being seen as merely competent to being seen as whole. It was the scariest and most liberating choice I had ever made.

Why We Hide

The Competence Prison

Professional success often requires maintaining an image of unwavering competence. We learn to project confidence even when we're uncertain, to appear composed even when we're struggling, and to seem like we have it all together even when we're unraveling inside.

This *competence prison* may serve us well in certain contexts, but it becomes a barrier to authentic leadership and genuine connection.

In high-achievement spaces, especially for women in male-dominated or performance-obsessed environments, vulnerability is often coded as weakness. We are conditioned to equate composure with credibility, to speak in certainties, conceal our questions, and armor ourselves in invincibility.

Beneath this impenetrable surface lies an estrangement so oppressive that it makes us entirely disconnected from ourselves and from others. Have you ever wondered whether the strength we perform is actually the very thing keeping us from authenticity? What if true power isn't being seen as perfect, but simply being seen?

We hide because we're afraid. That fear shrinks our lives, dulls our experiences, and traps us in cycles of regret. The thing is, we cannot avoid disappointment, sadness, and grief, just as we cannot shield ourselves from the full spectrum of feelings humans were destined to endure.

You might recall from Chapter Three, when we discussed *emotional regulation in high-stakes environments*, that fear will either make you shrink or sharpen you. Here, the fear of exposure made me shrink until I realized that real resilience doesn't mean hiding your humanity, but using it as a source of connection.

When we stop hiding, it's a pivotal moment that puts us one step closer to the life we've always dreamed of. We all know that our days are numbered and that the time we have on this earth is precious. So being courageous and allowing ourselves to be vulnerable should not be the exception to evasive and unwritten rules. On the contrary, we should all aspire to display the same level of vulnerability as the greatest minds of present and past generations.

A lot of our fears occur in our subconscious without us even realizing it. We are so accustomed to that nagging voice in the back of our minds telling us that we're forbidden from showing even the tiniest glimpse of emotion. It points out and emphasizes all our "weaknesses" as it narrates our day-to-day actions in the most negative of ways.

The Perfection Performance

High achievers often mistake perfectionism for excellence. We think that showing vulnerability, uncertainty, or a learning process will diminish our credibility or jeopardize our standing.

The Fears sound like this:

- If I admit I don't know something, will they question my expertise?

- If I show that I'm struggling, will they lose confidence in my leadership?

- If I reveal my growth process, will they see me as unstable or unreliable?

- If I share my authentic expression, will they judge me as
  unprofessional?

This mirrors the same inner tension we explored in Chapter Six, when
we talked about the *cost of identity misalignment*. Back then, I didn't
have the language for it, but I was living the very contradiction I now
teach leaders to break free from. We are finally privy to a level of self-
understanding and personal acceptance that had evaded us for so
long.

The Authority Addiction

When you're accustomed to being the expert, the advisor, the one with
answers, it becomes addictive. Your identity becomes tied to being
the person others turn to for solutions, and anything that threatens that
dynamic feels like a threat to your worth.

I was addicted to being the unshakeable one, the one who could
handle anything, the one who never showed weakness. Cancer forced
me to confront the reality that this identity was both unsustainable and
inauthentic.

This was my real-time *P.I.V.O.T.* moment, a point where my self-
perception had to be reshaped to make room for truth. I had to let go
of the role I was clinging to in order to grow into the leader I was
becoming.

Remember that you are capable of so much more than you imagine. Your inner self is waiting for you. As you step outside your limiting beliefs and hear that little voice trying to hold you back, gently remind yourself that trying is never in vain. It's the only way you will find your way back to yourself.

The Hidden Cost of Leading Behind a Mask

Leadership requires presence, not perfection. The most profound influence often emerges from having the courage to be seen.

I've learned that transformation, the life-changing kind, doesn't depend on flawless strategy. It requires radical honesty and the willingness to lead with both wisdom and vulnerability. People aren't inspired by someone who never stumbles. They're inspired by someone who shows them it's okay to stumble and *still move forward*.

And just like we discussed in Chapter Eight, where psychological *safety* was key to innovation, this kind of leadership creates an environment where people feel safe to contribute, collaborate, and even fail without fear of judgment.

Show them the unspoken liberty to be human, to heal, and to contribute even when you don't have it all together. This is the kind of leadership that cultivates emotional safety, and when you establish safety, you can finally have lasting transformation.

When Image Becomes the Leader

When you're constantly managing your image, you're performing, not leading.

Your decisions start to hinge on how they'll be perceived rather than on what's genuinely needed. Risks that could grow you or your team get avoided because they might reveal you're still learning. And in protecting the performance, you unintentionally shut the door on innovation and collaboration.

Throughout my journey of growth, I would never admit uncertainty in strategic meetings. If I didn't know something, I would deflect, research later, and circle back with a confident answer. It created the illusion of omniscience, but in reality, it cut me off from the very things leadership needs most: real-time problem solving, collective intelligence, and trust.

That's the truth about image-driven leadership: it creates distance between you and the very growth you're meant to foster. So technically you're in the driver's seat, but your mask is doing the steering. The shift begins when you stop curating perfection and start cultivating connection.

When Perfection Pushes People Away

When you lead from a place of performance instead of authenticity, people might admire your competence, but they can't connect with your humanity. The version of you they see is polished and controlled, but also untouchable. And when people can't access who you really are, they keep their own guard up, too.

The result? Professional relationships that are functionally effective but emotionally hollow. Colleagues who will work hard alongside you, but never truly know you. Respect without trust. Collaboration without connection.

I understand that in a world filled with engagements, commitments, and never-ending distractions, it's hard to pause for self-reflection when you're constantly chasing one thing after another. Especially with the endless stream of messages about who and what you "should" be. We're continuously bombarded with ideals of beauty, intelligence, humor, and confidence, and in trying to keep up, we lose ourselves.

Standing in your truth isn't about drastically changing who you are. On the contrary, it's about finding fulfillment from within. When you start being honest with yourself and others, you begin to live as the open-hearted, authentic person you were meant to be. Living with integrity, in both actions and communication, frees you not only from fear but from the constant need for external validation.

This kind of grounded self-awareness better equips you for adversity. When you know who you are, you have an anchor that holds steady when the road gets rough. A balanced outlook allows you to navigate unexpected detours and to understand that no matter what happens, you are home within yourself. When you are anchored in your truth, you have a compass to help you navigate life, set healthy boundaries, and take better care of yourself without guilt.

You've already tried accommodating everyone else's expectations and emotions, and it left you with exhaustion, anxiety, and an aching sense of emptiness. You know you can't keep living like this, drained by the weight of carrying what was never yours to carry. It's time to listen to yourself, reflect on your own needs, and step into the courage to unleash your extraordinary inner self.

Authenticity Is a Practice, Not a Performance

You've been wearing the mask for so long, it almost feels like part of your skin. Maybe you believed you had to carry yourself a certain way to be accepted. Maybe you thought you had to play different roles in different rooms just to belong.

Constantly shape-shifting to meet other people's expectations is exhausting. We all move through spaces where we feel like we can't be genuine, where honesty takes a backseat to politeness or self-preservation. In those moments, we tell people what they want to hear, even if it clashes with our values and our true nature.

Over time, as we move from one setting to the next, we start to adjust each version of ourselves until the line between the mask and the real

107

us blurs. Each time we bend or shrink to fit in, we lose a piece of who we are. Eventually, we wake up feeling far from the person we claim to be, wondering when we stopped living as ourselves and started living as an image.

We don't like to admit that the things we do and say reflect who we are. We convince ourselves we're detached from those acts because, in our minds, we had to behave that way to protect ourselves. We tell ourselves that someday, in the right place or with the right people, we'll drop the act. But that "right time" rarely comes, so instead, the mask becomes the identity.

Living inauthentically is not only exhausting but also tremendously limiting and deeply disheartening. It keeps us from unlocking our full potential. The source of that quiet unhappiness often hides in plain sight: our inability to embody our true essence in the everyday moments, not just the safe ones.

When we choose authentic and purposeful living, we give ourselves permission to be who we truly are. We begin to forge our own path, one aligned with our beliefs, values, and interests. As we grow and expand, we flourish into the person we were meant to be. We gain a clear vision of our purpose, our "why," and we know exactly how to pursue it.

The Transformation: From Image to Authenticity

The Moment of Choice

Stepping back into a high-visibility leadership role, I had to decide who I wanted to be as a leader. I could continue projecting the image of unwavering competence I had perfected for years, or I could integrate what I had learned about vulnerability, uncertainty, and human resilience from navigating my own real challenges in life and work.

One pivotal moment came during a presentation to senior leaders. Instead of delivering a standard briefing, I chose to share what my own experiences had taught me: the reality of leading through uncertainty, the critical role of emotional intelligence in crisis, and the power of authentic communication in building trust.

The response was profound. Instead of questioning my competence, they leaned in with interest. Instead of losing respect for my capabilities, they gained appreciation for my humanity. Instead of seeing weakness, they recognized a different kind of strength, one that could only come from leading without the mask.

This moment crystallized a truth I've been threading through every chapter: resilience without authenticity is just endurance. And endurance alone will not transform you or the people you lead.

Innovation Stifled by Image Protection

Authentic innovation requires the willingness to experiment, fail, and iterate publicly. But when you're protecting a perfect image, you avoid the messy process of genuine creativity and growth. Protecting a perfect image stifles that process.

For years, I played it safe professionally, choosing projects I knew I could execute flawlessly rather than challenges that would stretch my capabilities. *It felt safer to be seen as competent than to risk being seen in the process of becoming.*

But that's the problem: *safe isn't where growth happens*. Growth lives in the uncomfortable. This is where the *A.I.M. Method* from Chapter Five comes back into play, especially the *"Acknowledge"* and *"Identify"* stages. You can't choose growth without first identifying where you've been clinging to comfort.

Shifting from to-do to to-be is more than a productivity tweak, it's a declaration. It focuses your energy on who you want to become, not just what you need to complete.

Your to-be list shifts the question from *"What do I need to get done?"* to *"Who do I want to become?"* It centers your energy on the values you want to embody, the way you want to show up, and the parts of yourself you want to live out loud.

When you lead with to-be, your tasks become expressions of your identity, not just items to check off. That's when you stop chasing fulfillment and start living it.

Ask yourself:

- Who do I want to be in my relationships?
- Who do I want to be in my work?
- Who do I want to be when no one's watching?

The answers guide not just your next steps — but how you take them.

Check-In Moment: What Are You Still Hiding?

Let's be real for a moment. Take a breath. Put the book down if you need to. This is your space to answer honestly.

Reflection Prompts:

1. What part of your story are you still afraid to share?

2. What emotions have you buried in the name of professionalism?

3. What would it feel like to be seen-not as perfect, but as whole?

Remember:

You don't have to lead from the mountaintop.

You lead from the middle.

You lead from where you really are.

Because someone needs to see that success and struggle can exist in the same story and that strength is telling the truth about both.

Affirmations to Anchor In:

You are not too much.

You are not too messy.

You are not too unfinished.

You are a living, breathing example of what it looks like to evolve with both grace and grit.

Final Thought:

This is the kind of leadership the world needs more of. And it starts with you.

Chapter Twelve

Never Finished, Always Becoming

One day I got asked a question that stopped me cold: "Chief, how do you prepare for the unprepared-for?" I paused, not because I didn't know the answer, but because I finally understood something profound: **The most important education happens in the spaces between what we were taught and what life actually requires.**

There is a great liberation in surrendering the illusion of arrival. Having to be fully healed, altogether, or perpetually composed is a myth. We were told that with enough achievement, we would finally reach a place where everything clicked, a perfect point where education, career, and credentials would carry us through any challenge. But life's greatest challenges don't come with a syllabus or a strategic plan. They come as divorce papers, a biopsy result, a parent's decline, a child's crisis, a sudden loss, an identity shift you can't prepare for.

I believed that if I accomplished enough, I would finally reach a place where everything felt secure. But life, loss, and leadership taught me a deeper truth: there is no final state of completion, and that is not the failure of the journey. It's designed that way. We are not here to arrive. We are here to evolve. Again, and again.

I realized I was no longer the leader who believed that enough preparation could prevent all uncertainty. I had become someone who could navigate the unprepared-for with wisdom rather than just strategy.

This is what it means to be never finished, always becoming.

Michel de Montaigne said, *"The greatest thing in the world is to know how to belong to oneself."*

We spend years seeking approval from others, mentors, colleagues, friends, even people whose opinions shouldn't matter, and we live in an unconscious competition for validation. But the day we begin to appreciate ourselves for who we are is the day we begin to protect our energy from negativity, whether it's from our ego, our inner critic, or toxic voices around us.

The High Achiever's Reset Reality

Throughout this book, you've learned that change doesn't have to mean starting over. You've discovered that you can evolve without erasing your accomplishments, grow without abandoning your expertise, and transform without losing your professional credibility.

But here's what no one tells you about sustainable change for accomplished professionals: **you don't reset once and never need to again. You develop reset capacity.**

Life will continue presenting you with transitions that require everything you've learned here:

- Career pivots that challenge your identity

- Health challenges that demand new priorities

- Relationship changes that require emotional recalibration

- Industry disruptions that make your expertise obsolete

- Personal growth that outpaces your current professional context

- Global changes that shift the landscape of everything you've built

The question isn't whether you'll need to navigate change again. The question is: **Will you be able to reset practically without losing yourself in the process?**

Your Reset Infrastructure: What You've Built

1. Identity Integration Skills

You've learned to separate your worth from your performance, your identity from your role, and your value from your output. This doesn't mean these things don't matter; it means they don't define you completely.

Reset Application: When future changes threaten your professional identity, you have the skills to maintain your sense of self while adapting your approach.

Example: If industry changes make your current expertise less relevant, you can learn new skills without experiencing identity crisis because you know you are more than what you do.

2. The A.I.M. Navigation System

You have a practical, repeatable framework for moving through any transition: Acknowledge where you are, Identify who you're becoming, Move with aligned action.

Reset Application: Whether you're facing a career change, health challenge, relationship transition, or any other major shift, you have a systematic approach for navigating it.

Example: If your company restructures and eliminates your position, you can A.I.M. your way through it: acknowledge the reality and your emotions, identify what this transition reveals about your next evolution, and move strategically toward opportunities that align with your integrated self.

3. Mindset Update Capabilities

You understand how to update your mental operating system while keeping your core competencies. You can evolve your thinking without abandoning your intelligence.

Reset Application: When old success patterns start limiting your growth, you can update them systematically rather than being trapped by what worked before.

Example: If you've been promoted into a role that requires more collaborative leadership, but you've always succeeded through individual expertise, you can update your "expertise = identity" pattern to "expertise + collaboration = greater impact" without losing confidence in your abilities.

4. Professional Authenticity Integration

You've learned to be both competent and human, both professional and authentic, both accomplished and vulnerable when appropriate.

Reset Application: Future changes don't require you to choose between maintaining credibility and being genuine about your process.

117

Example: If you're navigating a personal crisis while maintaining professional responsibilities, you can establish clear boundaries and seek reasonable support without compromising your professional standing.

You Don't Have to Arrive to Be Ready

How we approach life's inevitabilities determines our fate. Being afraid to fail, unsure where to start, letting discouragement take hold, or focusing only on the negatives keeps you stuck in your comfort zone. If you want to get the most out of life, you must find ways to branch out, explore, and expand your horizons. After all, your limiting beliefs and other people's opinions don't have to dictate your reality. Learning to explore, experiment, and play is essential for personal growth, and you can do that by:

- Defining what you want without paying attention to unreasonable limits.

- Thinking about how the world will be if you don't act.

- Having someone to hold you accountable for your claims and promises.

Keep in mind that a failed experiment is just as valuable and essential as a successful one. Nelson Mandela said, "I never lose. I either win or learn." Regardless of the outcome, there is always a lesson to be learned. When you approach exploration with a mindset rooted in growth and abundance, rather than scarcity and self-preservation, you are bound to triumph despite the inevitable opposition.

Remember, obstacles are only as significant as you allow them to be. Stepping out of your comfort zone to explore, experiment, and play can be profoundly inspiring and invigorating. We cannot afford to deprive ourselves of this essential aspect of our existence, an aspect we crave and one vital to our happiness and well-being.

Many of history's most powerful discoveries and transformative breakthroughs began with experimentation and play. To experiment and play is to learn and thrive. Our natural curiosity and drive for adventure are intrinsic, and we should never suppress them, regardless of how unconventional the outcomes may be. While this path involves risk, embracing our curiosity allows us to learn more about ourselves and the world around us. By welcoming this side of ourselves, we also invite possibility, hope, and a deeper sense of meaning into our lives.

Certainty is not a prerequisite for transformation. You may still be carrying questions that resist tidy resolution, but that is not a sign of failure. It simply means you are alive and human. Wholeness is not the absence of doubt; it is the refusal to forsake yourself in the presence of it. Remember, healing is not performative. It is the kind of reckoning that allows you to meet your own gaze and, perhaps for the first time, recognize yourself.

This Isn't the End. It's the Reset.

The journey we've taken together through this book has given you something invaluable: **the ability to navigate change without losing yourself.** You've learned that reset does not mean restart, that evolution does not mean abandonment, and that growth does not threaten competence.

But most importantly, you've developed **reset capacity to rediscover your inner leader's mindset.**

What You Can Count On

You will face changes that require everything you've learned here. Your industry will evolve, your life circumstances will shift, your priorities will deepen, and your understanding of success will become more sophisticated.

You now have the tools to navigate those changes practically and sustainably. You don't have to start from scratch or lose your professional momentum. You can reset from integration rather than desperation.

You can help others understand that change is navigable. Your example of evolving without losing yourself gives others permission to grow.

While this doesn't mean that life will be easy from now on, it does mean that you have the tools to work with what you've got and improve the situation you're in. You won't magically have more time to accomplish what you've set out to do, but you will have more energy to tend to your priorities and find fulfillment in what you do and who you become.

Now, you can begin to invest more time in the things you've always wanted to try, the people you've always wanted to get to know better, and the communities you've always wanted to give more to. Everything that you've put on hold for the longest time is no longer impossible. You are in the driver's seat. You have the power to decide how your day goes and how your time is spent. Only you can decide how best to live your life, and only you can choose who you want to be and how you want to be seen.

There will be a time when you feel like you can't do it anymore. When it does, take a step back and examine the areas in your life in which you're overextending yourself. And most importantly, look back to where you came from.

Your past is your biggest source of inspiration. You are living proof of your own growth and evolution. You have probably gone through tougher times, and while that may not feel like consolation, you probably will again. Instead of throwing in the towel and declaring defeat, conjure up all those instances where you've shown tremendous strength and overcome the biggest challenges of your life.

Take pride in the person you've become today and in the time and effort you've invested in your development because that's what has gotten you here. Then summon your courage, face your fears, prepare to step up, and move forward.

The knowledge you have acquired from this book is your guiding light, enabling you to uncover a self that has long been buried under layers of metrics. When you combine all the small steps you take through your rituals, they accumulate to create a legacy you can be proud of. So raise your standards and always seek growth, because it is not what we possess that makes us happier, but who we become in the process.

You were never truly unprepared, only unequipped with the tools that went deeper than the job description. All you needed was permission to feel without explanation, to pause without guilt, and to pivot without shame.

This book was never meant to chart your path. It was meant to reflect your truth and invite you to lead from within.

So, if you find yourself still learning, healing, and figuring it out, that is good. That is the sacred labor of becoming, and there is no task more courageous.

Final Check-In: What Will You Carry Forward?

- What truth did this journey uncover for you?

- What are you letting go of so you can move forward in peace?

- Who are you becoming and how can you honor yourself in how you show up tomorrow?

You are not alone in this process.

You are not behind.

You are not broken.

You are just becoming.

And that, my friend, is the most educated you've ever been.

Acknowledgements

This book was never just mine; it was born from the lives, lessons, and love of so many people who shaped me along the way.

To my son, Jaece, your light reminds me why I keep showing up, even when life feels heavy. You are my joy, my mirror, my reason to keep choosing courage.

To my family, thank you for your steady love and for holding space for the unpolished parts of me.

To the mentors and leaders who shaped me, you taught me that leadership is not about titles or accolades, but about service, humility, and presence.

To my students, colleagues, and soldiers, you sharpened me. Your stories, resilience, and struggles live between these pages.

And to you, the reader, thank you for walking this journey with me. May these words remind you that your worth was never measured in credentials, productivity, or applause. It has always been in your ability to pause, breathe, and lead yourself home. And to remember that you are enough.

This is not just my story; it's an invitation to rediscover yours.

About the Author

Dr. Jada Jones has spent nearly two decades serving at the intersection of technology, leadership, and human development. As a U.S. Army Chief Warrant Officer, she led in environments where the stakes were nothing short of life or death. She became the leader people called when failure was not an option.

But her deepest lessons did not come from credentials or titles; they came from life itself. Confronting a breast cancer diagnosis, navigating burnout, and walking through seasons of grief revealed that external achievement means little without internal alignment. These experiences reshaped her understanding of leadership, teaching her that true capacity comes from within.

Jada's journey into wellness became as defining as her professional achievements, expanding her philosophy of leadership. By choosing health before crisis, she rebuilt her strength, shifted her identity, and embraced emotional intelligence as a way of living, not just leading. Today, she empowers quiet high achievers, professionals, and leaders to reconnect with their humanity while excelling in their purpose.

Her work is rooted in one simple but radical truth: credentials prove what you can do, but capacity determines who you can become. Through her writing, speaking, and coaching, Jada equips others to navigate transitions with clarity, resilience, and authenticity so they can live, lead, and thrive without losing themselves in the process.

Stay Connected

Thank you for reading!

I believe transformation begins with one step, and I'm honored to have shared part of this journey with you. If this book encouraged, challenged, or inspired you, I'd love to hear from you.

For speaking, coaching, or collaboration inquiries:

Email: [info@jadajonesspeaks.com]

Website: [www.jadajonesspeaks.com]

Let's stay connected:

Instagram: @iam_JadaJones

LinkedIn: www.linkedin.com/in/jadaljones

Podcast: IamTh3Proof

Sign up for updates & resources:

Visit [www.jadajonesspeaks.com/newsletter] to receive tools, journal prompts, and upcoming event news.

Remember: Who you are is how you win. Keep leading yourself forward

Resource Guide Page

The Thoughts That Steal Your Momentum

Exploring Cognitive Distortions and Reframing for Growth

Your mind is your greatest ally and sometimes your greatest obstacle. Cognitive distortions are sneaky thought patterns that distort reality, drain your energy, and keep you stuck. The good news? Once you learn to spot them, you can reframe them into thoughts that build momentum instead of stealing it.

Here are some of the most common distortions with reframes to reclaim your clarity, courage, and growth:

---

1. All-or-Nothing Thinking

The Thought That Steals Momentum: "If I don't get it perfect, it's a failure."

Reframe for Growth: "Progress, not perfection, builds momentum. Small wins compound."

---

2. Catastrophizing

The Thought That Steals Momentum: "This one mistake will ruin everything."

Reframe for Growth: "One setback is feedback, not a full stop. What can I learn here?"

3. Overgeneralization

The Thought That Steals Momentum: "I always mess this up. I'll never get it right."

Reframe for Growth: "This moment doesn't define me. I'm capable of change and growth."

---

4. Mind Reading

The Thought That Steals Momentum: "They must think I'm not good enough."

Reframe for Growth: "I can't control their thoughts. I can control how I show up."

---

5. Discounting the Positive

The Thought That Steals Momentum: "Sure, I did well, but anyone could have done that."

Reframe for Growth: "My wins count. Every success is evidence of my capability."

Techniques to Strengthen Your Growth Mindset

1. **Catch and Challenge:** Pause when you notice a distorted thought. Ask: *Is this fact or fear? What's another way to see this?*

2. **Reframe in Real Time:** Swap "I can't" for "I can learn." Replace "I failed" with "I'm still growing."

3. **Collect Evidence:** Keep a "Momentum Journal." Write down three small wins daily. Over time, it retrains your brain to see progress instead of lack.

4. **Ask Empowering Questions:** Instead of "Why me?" try "What can this teach me?" or "How can I use this to move forward?"

Your Go-To Growth Mindset Reset

A growth mindset means shifting from:

- *"I'm stuck"* → to *"I'm learning."*

- *"I failed"* → to *"I discovered what doesn't work yet."*

- *"I can't"* → to *"I can't, **yet**."*

💡 **Final Reminder:** Your thoughts don't just describe your reality, they create it. By reframing the patterns that steal your momentum, you reclaim your energy, focus, and resilience. This is how you shift from surviving life to shaping it

The A.I.M. Maintenance System

Weekly Professional A.I.M. Check-in

Monday - Acknowledge:

- What am I avoiding acknowledging about my current professional state?

- Where am I performing vs. being authentic this week?

- What truth about my development needs my attention?

Wednesday - Identity:

- How am I showing up professionally vs. who I'm becoming personally?
- What values guided my decisions this week?
- Where can I bring more authenticity to my professional role?

Friday - Movement:

- What aligned actions did I take this week?
- What opportunities did I miss to express my authentic self?
- How can I evolve while maintaining professional excellence?

Quarterly Integration Review

- How has my understanding of professional success evolved?
- What new aspects of my identity want professional expression?
- What adjustments need to happen in my approach to work?
- How am I modeling integrated living for others?

The Professional's A.I.M. Commitment

I acknowledge that my professional competence is only one dimension of my full capabilities.

I identify as a whole person whose authentic self can enhance rather than threaten my professional effectiveness.

I move with intention toward integration, understanding that my greatest contribution comes from leading with both expertise and authenticity.

I commit to professional evolution that honors both my achievements and my humanity.

The Three-Phase Integration Strategy

Phase 1: Internal Alignment (Months 1-3)

Goal: Get clear on who you're becoming before changing what you're doing

Focus: Internal work that doesn't threaten external stability

- Daily identity check-ins (Who am I showing as today?)
- Values-based decision making in small daily choices
- Boundary experiments that don't require major announcements
- Authentic voice practice in low-stakes situations

Professional Applications:

- Bring more of your authentic perspective to existing role
- Make decisions based on values, not just metrics
- Set small boundaries that honor your energy
- Speak up about issues that genuinely matter to you

Phase 2: Gradual Expression (Months 4-9)

Goal: Begin expressing your evolving identity within your current context

Focus: Testing authentic self-expression while maintaining professional credibility

- Micro-experiments in vulnerability and authenticity
- Strategic boundary setting based on your values

- Selective sharing of your growth journey with trusted people
- Professional choices that reflect your expanding identity

Professional Applications:

- Volunteer for projects that align with your authentic interests
- Bring your whole perspective to professional discussions
- Create innovations that reflect your evolving values
- Build relationships based on authenticity, not just for temporary fun

Phase 3: Integrated Living (Months 10+)

- Major decisions filtered through your authentic identity
- Professional choices that support your continued growth
- Leadership that models integration for others
- Career moves that honor both your competence and your authenticity

10 Questions to Help You Connect with Your Inner Self

Uncovering your inner self requires a great deal of introspection. You simply can't say, "I want to be happy" or "I want world peace." You have to dig deeper and follow up each statement with a "why" until you have your answer. So, how do you go about that?

You can start by answering the following questions. Consider this a self-reflection exercise, so sit back, take a deep breath, and get ready to delve deeper into your psyche. With each answer, you will get closer to finding common ground between your core values, your identity, and your passions.

- What were you passionate about as a child that you lost to the responsibilities of adulthood?

- What do you truly enjoy doing that makes you forget the world around you?

- What is something that you make excuses for not doing that truly scares you?

- What is the number one item on your bucket list?

- If you had all the money in the world, how would you choose to fill your time?

- What are your unique strengths and talents?

- What drives you to wake up in the morning and persevere during the day?

- What kind of discussions do you have with the people close to you?

- What core values guide most of your actions?

- What is most important to you?

Practical Mindset Maintenance for Busy Professionals

The 5-Minute Morning Reset

1. **Acknowledge** where yesterday's old patterns showed up

2. **Affirm** one updated belief you're practicing today

3. **Align** your top three priorities with your evolving values

4. **Action** commit to one behavior that reflects your updated mindset

The Professional Vulnerability Framework

Level 1: Process Transparency Share your thinking process, not just your final answers.

Instead of: "Here's the solution we should implement" **Try:** "Here's how I've been thinking about this challenge and the approach I'm recommending"

Level 2: Learning Admission Acknowledge when you're developing new skills or understanding.

Instead of: Pretending you know everything about a new area **Try:** "I'm developing expertise in this area and here's what I've learned so far"

Level 3: Values Integration Connect your professional decisions to your personal values and purpose.

Instead of: Making decisions based only on metrics and strategy **Try:** "This approach aligns with both our business objectives and my values around sustainability"

Level 4: Human Acknowledgment Recognize the human impact of professional challenges and changes.

Instead of: "This restructuring will improve efficiency" **Try:** "This restructuring will improve efficiency, and I understand it creates uncertainty that affects real people"